Occultism

The Ultimate Guide to the Occult and Alchemy

(Protect Your Home and Family and Attract What You Desire)

Arletha Macon

Published By **Simon Dough**

Arletha Macon

All Rights Reserved

Occultism: The Ultimate Guide to the Occult and Alchemy (Protect Your Home and Family and Attract What You Desire)

ISBN 978-1-77485-508-9

No part of this guidebook shall be reproduced in any form without permission in writing from the publisher except in the case of brief quotations embodied in critical articles or reviews.

Legal & Disclaimer

The information contained in this ebook is not designed to replace or take the place of any form of medicine or professional medical advice. The information in this ebook has been provided for educational & entertainment purposes only.

The information contained in this book has been compiled from sources deemed reliable, and it is accurate to the best of the Author's knowledge; however, the Author cannot guarantee its accuracy and validity and cannot be held liable for any errors or omissions. Changes are periodically made to this book. You must consult your doctor or get professional medical advice before using any of the suggested remedies, techniques, or information in this book.

Upon using the information contained in this book, you agree to hold harmless the Author from and against any damages, costs, and expenses, including any legal fees potentially resulting from the application of any of the information provided by this guide. This disclaimer applies to any damages or injury caused by the use and application, whether directly or indirectly, of any advice or information presented, whether for breach of contract, tort, negligence, personal injury, criminal intent, or under any other cause of action.

You agree to accept all risks of using the information presented inside this book. You need to consult a professional medical practitioner in order to ensure you are both able and healthy enough to participate in this program.

Table of Contents

INTRODUCTION 1

CHAPTER 1: WHAT EXACTLY IS AN OCCULT? 5

CHAPTER 2: FULFILLMENT DREAMS, END RESULT OF SUCCEED 24

CHAPTER 3: THE WITCH WITHIN: INVOKING YOUR INNER WITCH 27

CHAPTER 4: SCIENCE OF MAGIC 57

CHAPTER 5: THE BUILDING OF YOUR ALTAR 59

CHAPTER 6: KEEPING A GRIMOIRE OR BOOK OF SHADOWS 76

CHAPTER 7: BREAKING THE CODE OF DIVINATION PSYCHIC POWERS 103

CHAPTER 8: THE IN VOCATIONAL POWER OF INVOCATION 121

CHAPTER 9: CRYSTAL MAGIC AND ALCHEMY 136

CHAPTER 10: DESIGNING YOUR RITUALS AND SPELLS ... 154

CHAPTER 11: TOOLS OF THE CRAFT 170

CONCLUSION 182

Introduction

Vashikaran is a branch of Hindu magic that deals with controlling the mind of the desire person to make them perform as we wish. It's a tantric technique to influence the desires of a person. While there are a variety of remedies astrological that can solve issues related to love or marriage, friendship, and many other relationships, it is observed that traditional astrology remedies take long to show the results, however Vashikaran is one such powerful remedy that shows results quickly and is totally safe.

Through Vashikaran it is possible to attract the person you want to towards the person you want to influence. Sometimes we don't express our thoughts to the wanted person, and we want a magic to occur that will make the person will himself or herself is interested in us will contact us. This is where Vashikaran will help you. Vashikaran mantras when done in an precise method, then the person will reach out to you and fulfill your wish.

Sometimes, marital conflicts can be difficult to resolve and the situation gets worse for both the spouses. This is where Vashikaran is a guaranteed solution for enhancing the relationship between the couple and the in-laws. Through Vashikaran you can turn your enemies your friend and bring your boss more manageable and become the center of attention at meetings and social gatherings. Your charisma and charm will increase numerous times. Vashikaran is done through a ritualistic method or by wearing an piece of Vashikaran like a locket, yantra or other.

There are a variety of methods for doing the Vashikaran. It's all dependent on the individual need to know the purpose and method they would like to make use of Vashikaran.

In many cases, it is observed in our culture the marriage couple's relationship tends to grow bitter! Sometimes, men are caught by the snares of a foreign children and women by his wife who is unable to remember! In the same way, women and men forget that their husbands are being sucked into the trap! The husband and wife, not just in the father-son bond is made bitter through Vidweshanam (Hatred) and so on.

The use of these spells to remove bitterness. the most simple way that can be used to troubleshoot any of them. In addition, the mantra that you can use to captivate both your servant and master! Additionally, you can captivate lovers and the purpose for being relatives is possible!

Vashikaran will help you in times of

* You are in love with a specific person but you aren't able to offer him or her a date

* Your boyfriend or girlfriend isn't at all

* Your partner has changed their behavior or has an extramarital relationship.

* You are unhappy with the behavior of your Mother or Father Law

* Your Mother or Father isn't at all ready to marry you.

Your manager or staff is not working with you or you're unhappy with the office environment.

* Your friend from the past has gotten away from you.

* Your adversaries are creating difficulties for you.

The astrological remedies are not effective for you.

You're looking to build an attractive and appealing personality

* Would you like to be successful in the world of politics

* Would like to end divorce or divorce-related situations

There are many other uses for this secret knowledge of witchcraft and occult sciences from Ancient Hindu tradition. Make sure to use it correctly to reach your goals efficient and smooth manner, we provide safety guidelines that are suitable for beginners too.

Chapter 1: What Exactly Is An Occult?

The term "occult" is derived from the late 15th century Latin "occultus" and the middle French "occultus" along with the Middle French "occulte," being the past participle of "oculere." All is interpreted to refer to "clandestine or secret, hidden and hidden or to be hidden from the public eye."

The occult was associated with studies of the paranormal, such as magic, alchemy and astrology precognition, telekinesis metaphysics, and necromancy during the 16th century. The first known usage of the term "occultism" found in English writings is in an article entitled "A A Few Questions for Hiraf" which was published 1875 in the Spiritual Scientist, an American spiritualist magazine. An Russian immigrants and the Theosophist founder named Helena Blavatsky wrote this article during her time within America. United States. In the broadest sense, theosophy is a range of paranormal beliefs and practices that are a mix of mysticism, magic, and spirituality. It's also connected to the paranormal, such as parapsychology, extrasensory vision, psychokinesis, psychometry and psychometry.

The opposite of occultism is apocalypse. It is derived taken from the Greek word "apokalyptein," a spiritual word that refers to the revelation or disclosure. This is the reason why religions consider occultism to be the opposite of God. The occultist has a devotion to the study of spiritual wisdom that goes beyond the physical world and the tentacles of science.

Numerous opinions and speculations are available concerning the practice and understanding of mystic entities and otherworldly forces. These beings, powers, and beliefs, mostly supernatural and divinatory, have existed for centuries and are recorded in the past however, there are significant differences in their appearance and view.

This field of study is currently under scrutiny and criticism because it suggests certain practices and subtleties that are not in line with the common perception of the normal." To the average person the main aspect of occultism lies in the experts' alleged ability to alter or manipulate natural laws and ethics, for their own, or someone else's benefit.

Anthropologists say it's impossible to differentiate between magic and religion which is the main ingredient of the occult beliefs. This is true for different religious sects within different societies. Although, this belief is not true as the majority of religious communities view natural moral laws as a clear and unambiguous matter in their own way.

Evolution of the Occult

The 20th, 19th and 19th century stories about the supernatural within the West has influenced the current understanding of the occult. Between 16th and 17th centuries, there saw people who believed that there existed supernatural entities and forces. The existence of forces that were beyond human control provided comfort for some, but pain, terror and even death for some. Many occult practitioners ruled supreme due to their power to control their psychic abilities.

The events that transpired resulted in the holy inquisition as well as texts such as Malleus Maleficarum, which served to end many lives, if more than thousands Satanists witches, occultists, as well as others "heretics." It was the persecuting and torture of occultists resulted in an increase in the number of false religious clerics' efforts to mislead people with false claims of miracles and the alleged virtues of virtue. In the 16th century and 17th, saw an intense examination of controversial supernatural events beginning with artifacts and more recently, witch hunter's plight.

Western occultism is a long-standing hidden belief that underlies every occult ritual. The hidden philosophy is rooted in magickal alchemy as well as Hellenistic magic on one side as well as Jewish spirituality on the other hand. The main source for Hellenistic Magic is the book composed by Hermes Trismegistus. This text is known as The Corpus Hermeticum, and this treatise is filled with astrology, gnosis magic, alchemy, as well as other mystic sciences that promote spiritual regeneration. The doctrines of the treatise were integral to the development of Wicca as well as modern neo-paganism along with Western magic.

Jewish mysticism is further fueled by the Kabbalah that is comprised of esoteric teachings mysticism. The Zohar is written in middle-age Hebrew and Aramaic is a compilation of mystical comments of the Torah and forms the Kabbalah's core. Jewish metaphysical thinking was well-known to European scholars during the Middle Ages and was associated with the Corpus Hermeticum through the Renaissance. The subsequent Hermetic-Kabbalistic tradition was known as Hermeticism. It was later incorporated into an idea and a practice of magic (the latter was regarded as positive and natural magic in contrast against that of "negative magic" provided by sorcery or witchcraft).

The alchemical science was a part of Hermeticism. It was further developed by the rise of Rosicrucianism during the early 17th century. The Rosicrucians were an undercover society that utilized symbols of alchemy and passed on the arcane wisdom of the past to their followers, creating an alchemical method of spirituality that lasted well beyond the development of scientific theories and allowed Hermetism to flourish through The Age of Enlightenment (1715 - 1789).

At the turn of 18th-century, Freemasons were able to adopt occultism because they couldn't find an appropriate occult doctrine within Freemasonry. These esoterically inclined individuals remained as Hermeticism's lone scholars and as occult organizations in Continental Europe into the 19th century and into the 19th century, when religious cynicism led to an increase in the rejection of Orthodox doctrines by the modern. This was then a catalyst to a subsequent quest for redemption via any other method, which included the practice of occultism.

As Protestantism was able to lose its the significance of its culture and social status, and scientific research and the study of nature phenomena gained traction and a general distrust was born. In the late 17th century this distrust led to the birth of Deism which was a philosophical school that reinforced the idea of God was the one who created natural laws.

The doctrine of Deism was only available to certain prominent and influential members of society, such as George Washington, Benjamin Franklin and other founders of America. The 19th century brought the mysticism-based view doubtful the foundation for "free thoughts." Freethinkers were influential in all kinds of theological and academic thought in the era. These events involved preachers engaged in heated discussions with atheists who were confirmed as believers and theologians who proved God's existence and missionaries increasing their efforts to influence the unbelievers.

With the reemergence of mysticism during the late 19th century occultism was unable to gain traction in the academic circles, even though it had an impact on famous artists such as Wassily Kandinsky and Austin Osman Spare and writer William Butler Yeats from time to time.

With all this, it's likely that the definition of occultism has changed from being obscured by mystery and hidden information to the uninitiated being a subject of different interpretations and myths. In the fierce argument between religious and free-thinkers, a small group of people who prefer to be known as "Spiritualists" offer an alternative view. They argue that the distinction between the present and the future is a speculation that we have invented and that everything we know and unknowable, is part of the universe. Spiritualists sought help from seers to gain access to the spiritual realm to relay messages that couldn't be received through conventional methods.

The seers were able to channel a range of psychic phenomena, which pointed towards the existence of unobserved forces operating in the physical realm that were not documented by the scientific organizations that were prevalent in the time. As a result, with the advent and growth of spiritualism certain academics with connection to religion and methods of observation believed to be utilized to study ghostly sightings, specifically in regards to ghosts, apparitions and ghosts. The concept was born in Britain's Ghost Club in 1862, and a number of investigations were conducted regarding supernatural sightings throughout the following two years. The year 1882 was when New Age researchers started the London Society for Psychical Research to investigate the happenings of supernatural seances, as well as other supernatural phenomena.

The period of time from 1882 to 1939 -- the start in the second world war--denoted an uneasy alliance with psychic studies and Spiritualism. Spiritualism , and other branchings (primarily Theosophy) revealed psychic phenomena that researchers studied and studied. They realized that these phenomena when they were confirmed, would have profound implications in understanding the world and the machinations that it enacts.

A wealth of information was gathered in both negative and positive ways. Evidence proving a variety of supernatural phenomena that support the mortal-spirit connection was collected. In parallel, it was found that the vast majority of information collected by mediums like the mind over matter and telekinesis materializations was often fake. The increasing use of tricks even when seers are regarded as authentic, led to an issue.

The events led people to doubt the credibility of Spiritualism. Although it didn't declare each occultist or medium fraudulent, it suggested that the occult world provided shelter to crooks and facilitated their practice, even with clear evidence of fraud. It also categorizes psychic researchers that produced conclusive evidence as untrustworthy or lackadaisical. They could also be aides to fraudsters who disguise themselves as mediums.

This was the most significant of the writings from Lewis Spence and Nandor Fodor. The latter published a book titled Encyclopedia of Occultism and Parapsychology that discussed psychic phenomena from the Spiritualist view, while expressing his wish for scientists to find the methods to verify supernatural phenomena.

The Fodor's Encyclopedia of Psychic Sciences was published in the decade following this. The book acknowledged the existence of fakery and deceit in Spiritualism however, Fodor believed in the evidence that was gathered by famous psychic researchers as well as other colleagues.

Half a century later, after Fodor and Spence's books, the metaphysical and occult have been given a fresh look. A face that is backed through"New Age. "New Age" movement.

The concepts that surround Theosophy, Spiritualism, and supernatural phenomena have been radically changed by the development of parapsychology. The incorporation into The Parapsychological Association into the American Academy for Scientific Advancement has allowed the public to see transparency and honesty in research in the mystical field by the scientific community as parapsychologists became more conventional and renounced the majority of findings from earlier research.

New Age Occultism

In the past the occult and deviances from natural law were attributed to unknown entities, souls of the deceased and other undiscovered entities. Rituals were performed to stave off misfortune, gain insight of future or past events and to accumulate wealth, inflict harm to the enemies of one's and bring spirits and entities to life. In the past, indigenous cultures have associated rituals of the occult with conjurers, shamans and other practitioners possessing supernatural powers.

In the last decade of the 20th century, about 1970 there was a rise in the practice of occult. 1980 was the year of what is now known as the New Age Coalition. The increasing interest in metaphysical ideas and the supernatural phenomena led to the development of channeling using crystals, the belief in angels and rituals for exorcism. No matter what the latest trends are, the field of parapsychology has been established in the mainstream of society in ways that no one would have anticipated in the 1950s.

Following the fall of the Roman Empire in the Middle Ages The early Church attempted to regulate the populace. The strategy of the Church was to scold those who were not conforming to the Church's guidelines. Although more and more people embraced Christianity but the old methods were still practiced with absolute secret. In the past all practice that was not within the

Christian beliefs was considered a dark and occult practice. The Church determined that any ritual, science or art practice that was not rationally understood was classified as the occult.

The mystic arts might have scared some people however, they were not the only ones who were scared. Middle Ages saw the separation of occultism and religion, as well as its opposition to traditional religions. A lot of rituals and spells from those of the Middle Ages are based on the pre-Christian religions of Mediterranean countries.

The way one views the possibility of supernatural events and the occult depends on one's religion or philosophical view. For example, Allan Kardec's theories on Spiritism is a subset of Spiritualism which believes in Reincarnation. Spiritism as well as Spiritualism are basically religions that both confirm supernatural events in the Bible and confirming the supernatural as being true and legitimate.

The metaphysical remains regarded by many as "occult" even to this day. From it was the Middle Ages, occultism has been a derogatory term applied to a myriad of supernatural groups or associations that all share various commonalities, such as the practice of rituals or practices; training of members in the historyof the group; the secret knowledge as well as philosophical concepts that guide the members.

The New Age movement has refuted these assertions by reforming the occult. Tarot reading, astrology palmistry, numerology scrying, rune casting have been categorized as counseling techniques, while Wiccans have gathered to debunk witchcraft and discredit these as fanaticism based on religion.

Groups interested in the subject aligned themselves with the latest blends of occult science, such as Hyperanism. Certain groups embrace Theosophy which is a blend that combines Western as well as Eastern occultism. Other groups opt for Spiritualism that allows communication between those who live and those who die through an intermediary.

Branchings of Occultism

The Church's values remain the basis for defining Neo-occultism as a. In the Complete Evangelism Guidebook categorizes the general practice of occultism in three categories:

* Divinatory practices: This section of occult research seeks to uncover secrets, typically about the near or distant future by using psychic readings and other mystical techniques. Divinatory tools include palmistry scrying with crystals , tea leaves and various divination tools.

* Paganism * Paganism: It is commonly known as Neo-Paganism and is distinct from the vibrant revival of the ancient Paganism that began during the late 19th century. The 1960s witnessed the emergence of Animism which is the belief that there is the soul of a living being to objects creatures, people, or even objects that are not living. The Animism religion is a tribute to the gods of the past such as Gaia and Mother Earth.

* Spiritism: Spiritism and Spiritualism are often used interchangeably however there are distinct differences between these religions. In the beginning, Spiritualism began with the Fox sisters, Leah, Margaretta, and Catherine in 1848. It was the French academic Hippolyte Leo Denizard Rivail (also called Allan Kardec) started

Spiritism in 1850. Spiritism is an aspect of Spiritualism. Spiritualists as well as Spiritists believe that discarnate entities as well as humans are able to communicate and keep relationships alive. The only Spiritists are believers in the concept of reincarnation and the development of souls. However, Spiritualists claim reincarnation is impossible since it shuts off the connection between our living and the departed. Spiritualism is a belief that there is a God and the existence of God, however Spiritism is not a religion with a formal basis. Both are comparable because both have their roots in the occult, and both require an belief in the paranormal. Spiritualism was a popular belief in the modern era due to the increasing popularity of séances in the 1890s until 1920.

Myths About Occultism

In the past the occult has been painted with a brush stroke of evil and illegal practices. Here are some of the most popular myths that are a part of occultism.

* Science is part of the Occult Science was largely misunderstood throughout the Middle Ages, and for this reason, it was

labeled an occult practice among religious sects. The interplay between chemicals and elements, or between objects and substances were not understood, and they were branded "magic." They considered themselves "practitioners who practiced Earth the art of magic" since they worked with altering and controlling natural elements. Alchemists were called "witches" as well as "warlocks" since they had the ability to alter elements and metals with heat and other awe-inspiring techniques.

The *cult and Occult are the same thing Many consider Christianity as a religious cult in itself. Certain groups which were once considered cults have over time and socially changed to become religious organizations. Examples include those of the Seventh Day Adventists, led at one point by Ellen White, and the Mormons which were headed by Joseph Smith.

Some believe that the term "cult" can be nothing more than an insulting term used to describe new religions and their followers. Cults are religious groups with established beliefs and power that revolves around an individual leader. This fervent following requires an entire group of people who have a high degree of dedication, and also commitments that aren't like other groups.

However the occult can be described as an unspoken system of convictions and beliefs that don't require a large group of individuals. Anyone can become an occultist. Occultism is the pursuit of the truth, whereas the cults do not seek the pursuit of knowledge. The use of "cult" as well as "occult" in the same sentence is a dangerous misconception and is a false generalization.

"Occultism" Synonymous with Satanism The common belief of the occult is to believe the belief that everyone who is Satanists are occultists, and the reverse is true. This is a fact that dates back to the church's classification of the term "occult", as well as other ancient practices of the secret world. Theistic Satanism is a religion that views Satan and Lucifer as a neutral supernatural being worthy of reverence and worship. Satanists believe that their religion is an avenue of spiritual understanding, individuality of thinking and self-development. The Church's position regarding occultism has been criticized as sanctimonious and insincere, especially when it is viewed by the Biblical Christian Ethereal Lens of the Library. The Church has claimed an unending string of supernatural powers, such as demon exorcisms, the gift of tongues, powers of prophecy, and the resurrection of the dead. In light of this the Church should be viewed as occult and compared to Satanism.

Chapter 2: Fulfillment Dreams, End Result

Of Succeed

When we look at the contents of our minds, it is quite evident that our mind is constantly searching for something that isn't there. It is no doubt that there's a gap caused in our minds that is always in search of something, and it's like an never-ending cycle. Desire begets desire . Once we've got one thing, we begin to crave for other. Now success must be understood in this sense. We desire something, and if it is accomplished, then we are successful , but when it isn't, there is a part of a desire in our brain.

It is interesting that whether or not we accomplish anything or not, the aspect of desire is present within our own consciousness. If the desire is able to be cured by the practice of meditation and meditation, then I believe that whether we accomplish something or not, we will be able to calm the rumbling in our minds.

We are left with only two choices . Or, we can achieve what we really want , or we can sooth the perpetual need that runs through our brains. The problem with achieving your desires is that the freedom of mind is very short-lived in nature. Finding the source of the desire within us will allow us to be free for a lengthy period of time. Be aware of your inner self. It is the root of everything we desire from our lives. Knowing our own inner self opens the way to the world to abundance for us, and that is the biggest success of our lives.

As the name of the book the the subtle science behind success, we must try to understand the mechanisms that lead to satisfaction of our desires. The mind also is able to fulfill all our desires. A mind that has been developed through practicing meditation is able to meet all the needs that arise in him. He can achieve whatever he desires. The only thing that is required is to look inwards toward the expanded consciousness inside our own minds. We believe that, at the level of the mind, we can expand or contract our self. We are able to increase or decrease the mind-body vibrations that occur inside our own minds. The mind isn't a static state of being for us .

It is able to be transported to higher levels that exist for us . And that is the purpose of our higher existence.

In order to understand the nature of desires, it is important to be aware of the different layers of our mind operating inside our minds. The first is thoughts and then there is the sophisticated world of visualization or imagination inside our minds. A lot of successful people in the world have employed imagination to create their success . They have focused their attention on the things they wish to accomplish in their lives . This powerful visualization has resulted by perseverance . In the yogic or meditative realm, the results are instantaneous.

Chapter 3: The Witch Within: Invoking Your Inner Witch

Witchcraft is an art, science and an art of living all in one. Not a thing that needs to be burned alive for, the number witches of recent times has risen dramatically. According to the American Academy of Religions recognizes Wicca and witchcraft as legitimate practices. In the Pentagon 1,51 soldiers from the Air Force and 354 in the US marines have been practicing the craft. According to the American Department of Defense allows Wiccan soldiers to declare their beliefs on dog tags.

Some Signs There are Signs You Might Be a Witch

1. You possess a sixth sense that's always right and can be a manifestation of your desires or someone's presence.

2. You are blessed with an aura of healing or calm.

3. You are motivated by the desire to serve or help people. You might be volunteering in soup kitchens, pushing to make a difference

across the globe and always putting other peoples' needs ahead of your own.

4. You're the odd child, the oddball or perhaps the black sheep within your family. You might be feeling like an outsider looking at the world through the windows of your home, or are struggling to meet new people; and are often exhausted from by being surrounded by other people's energy all day long.

5. Dream in high-definition and these dreams aren't mere figments of your imagination as everyone else's. They have a deeper significance, similar to the messages of celestial guidebooks.

6. There are times when you hear voices or whispers coming from sources that are not visible. If you've ruled out schizophrenia or other mental illnesses, you could be an clairaudient. You can choose to develop this ability or to stifle it.

7. It is impossible not to feel a feeling of connection to the natural world. You're at peace with it, and are part of it. The majority of witches are aware of the cycle of life as well as how everything is interconnected.

8. You're extremely self-aware and show more empathy than most people and you are the perfect example of walking a mile in someone else's shoes.

9. You are more tactful than anyone else because you seem to know what to say to someone you love who is in need, and keep away from tension.

10. People who don't know you are always wanting to know your opinion or turning to you to seek guidance. Everyone has a "ride or perish."

11. There is a chance that you have experienced an experience of near-death that put you in a position in which you're more conscious of the mysteries of Earth as well as the universe beyond.

12. You love your company and don't hesitate to make demands. You enjoy people, but know that you need your own time to grow spiritually and be in touch to your higher self.

13. Find the solutions to the puzzles of life in nature. You can feel at ease and energized in natural spaces such as the beach, woods or in the park. Your body and your moods

are in tune with the phases of moon or the changing seasons.

14. You're a sponge, taking in all information about the supernatural and ancient healing techniques. You could also be awed by the marvels of the universe.

15. You are in love with the animals (even animals that are wild) and they attract you. Strays frequently stay with you at home. It is possible to talk with them.

16. There are messages and insights in antiques, energies or the appearances of your daily life.

17. You feel more energy and auras more than the majority of people.

18. Your wishes are often are fulfilled even if you say them in anger.

19. You may be referred to in the form of "old soul."

20. It's hard to resist your love to collect objects. You're a packrat always collecting antiques, bones, crystals, feathers, shells, and various items that contain earth's energy. Items that no "normal" person would find interesting.

21. You are fascinated by the idea of death and the events that occur after death, frequently you feel like your loved ones are with you sending love and light in some way or other.

If any of these symptoms are in your personality If so, congratulations! You could be a witch.

Basic Witchcraft Terms

As with all fields the witchcraft field has its own language. The list below isn't exhaustive however, here are some of the terms that you have to be familiar with in order to be able to walk the path.

Altar: It is a high-pitched surface used for rituals and religious services like the worship of God as well as Goddesses, singing, or casting spells. Altars are typically covered with an ornamental cloth that is decorated with magical images and ceremonial objects such as candles as well as incense, ash, the chalice, liquids, symbols that represent the elements of four and so on. The altar is a central part of Wicca and Pagan religious traditions altars are not utilized for blood sacrifices.

Amulet: It is an inanimate object that has been infused with magic that protects the wearer from harm illnesses, sickness, and bad luck. The term "amulet" is derived in the Old Latin "amoletum," which means "line to defend."

Ankh Ankh Egyptian symbol of renewal, life and immortality. It is usually created into talismans and amulets to ward off bad luck and bring good luck.

Arrow Position An stance that is similar in stance to Eastern yoga asanas and mudras. The stance is commonly used practiced in Pagan or Wiccan rituals, where participants put their feet together and lift their arms straight over their heads with their palms in contact.

Athame An Athame: A ritual knife for witches for use in ceremonies. It is generally constructed of steel or iron and double-edged, with an hilt of black. Athames are a symbol of phallic meaning. The chalice that it is poured into signifies the union of female and male energies. It is a symbol of the element of air in magic and rituals. It is used for marking circles of magic, but never to be used for cutting. If it is necessary cut or cut-off, they employ an oblique.

Auto-da-fe can be described as Portuguese meaning "act in belief." The ceremony was formal ceremony in the public domain, held during both the Spanish and Portuguese governments during the time of the inquisition prior to the pronouncement of judgement. The punishment of this period was in different types however the most well-known was the death penalty.

A Year and one Day: This is the standard duration of time used in many Pagan rituals. In Wicca it's the usual amount of time for an initiate to study in order before moving on to the next stage of witchcraft.

Baba Yaga: Also called the "bony legged one" Baba Yaga is a famous Slavic witch, who is known to offer healing. Contrary to how she's depicted there is much more to Baba Yaga than meets the eye. She is a balance between death and rebirth, dark forest as well as sickness and dying and also brings rejuvenation of healing, healing, and profound wisdom. Her power is most intense during autumn, beginning close to Mabon or Samhain.

Befana The good witch of Italian folklore that is known for bringing presents to the children during Epiphany. Other countries also have Santa Claus.

Bell, Book, and Candle It is believed that this originated from the Catholic practice of disqualifying witches. The sound of the bell symbolizes death toll. Also, the closing of the Book (the Bible) and the burning of a candle signify the removal of one's soul from God's view.

Besom: It is also known as Witch's Broom. The bristles are laid out in a circular pattern and composed of twigs and attached to sticks.

Black Book: Now called the Book of Shadows, following Gardner's influence, witches first made use of "the "Black Book" to record recipes or chants, as well as spells.

Blessed be: A well-known Wiccan salutation, which is sometimes shortened in "BB."

Bodkin Pins: pin-like instruments that were employed in torturing witches. Bodkins were employed in the witch-burning scandal in which witches were accused of offering their lives to the Devil for power and having an image (the Satan's Mark) upon their bodies. According to the government and the Church, which was oppressive the Devil's mark meant that the witch would not feel pain and would never be bleeding. Bodkins were employed to poke witches until the marks in their body were found.

Bolline: A knife with a crescent-shaped design with white handles that are popular with Druid and Wiccan practices for making cuts for cutting herbs, writing symbols on wax or wood.

The Book of Shadows: Shortened to "BOS," the renowned Gerald Gardner introduced this. The witch creates it using leather or soft cloth as its cover, and parchment or hand-made papers for its pages. It's a collection of chants, rituals, beliefs, spells and morals that are meant to help a witch practice their art. It was traditionally the form of a single copy that was owned by the Priestess or High Priest However, these days other coven members also possess an individual Book of Shadows, which must be destroyed after the owner's death.

The Cakes and Wines are also referred to as ale and cakes. This is a leisurely sharing of refreshments at the end of the ritual. The Priestess and High Priest should first taste their food prior to sharing the food with the other participants.

Cantrip: Scottish phrase used to describe minor magic spells. It may also refer on spells with forward and reverse.

Cauldron: A kettle made of iron or pot to burn incense, lighting fires, magic feasts and potions and other magical drinks. Nowadays, witches make use of domestic pots and vessels that they adore for the purpose of bringing magic.

Censer: Small container to burn incense, herbs and chemical substances to cleanse the air, increase energy levels, and summon spirits prior to rituals.

The Chalice, also known as the Goblet symbolises the element water. It's used to contain wine or water that is sacrificed to God. If it is upright the chalice symbolizes an open womb waiting to receive or contain. A chalice that is inverted signifies the rebirth of the womb and the realization.

Circe It is an Greek sorceress who is famous for her magical enchantments. She is famous for her ability to turn Odysseus's men to swine. In many stories her mother is Hecate who is the goddess of patronage of magic.

Cingulum is Latin to mean "belt" also known as "girdle." Cingulum is an unsecrated witch's cord typically nine feet long. It is used to signify an altar and is usually worn around the waist of the witch as an karate belt, to signify their rank or the level of initiation.

Conjure Bags or Charms Conjure Bags or Charms: These are pouches with drawstrings placed on the neck or around the waist. They contain mysterious objects of all kinds including bones as well as sulfur and salt as well as nails, plants and gems. They are very popular in the practice of voodoo.

Cookbook Witch is a witch who attempts to learn how to use magic by reading an instructional book.

Coven A collective consisting of Wiccans or witches whose numbers range between three and twenty however the standard number is thirteen.

Cowan The uninitiated which means anyone who isn't Wiccan or witch.

The Craft Name is a brand new name that a witch is given upon her beginning. Most craft names revolve around favorite deities.

The crossing of the Bridge Funeral.

Crown: A narrow strip made of gold or silver with the moon's crescent in the front. Together with the cingulum it signals rank in the coven.

The Degree (of Witchcraft) The four degrees of witchcraft include a neophyte, or first degree middle stage or the second degree, the second-middle stage and fully-fledged, or the third degree. Each degree is marked with a distinctive symbol, an inverted triangle, pentagram, as well as a triangle that is on top of the pentagram. Witches sometimes draw these symbols in the form of their names.

Devotee: Someone who dedicates their time to study within coven.

Deosil: Clockwise according to Gaelic orthography. It is a signifying a direction that runs from East toward West. It is also known as the prosperous path and is the most common direction for casting spells by witches, ritual circle or dance.

Diana: Roman Goddess considered as the goddess of witches. Artemis has been her Greek sister.

Drawing down the Moon: A fundamental ritual in the Wiccan tradition in which the High Priestess is transformed into the Goddess who is incarnated. The ritual is carried out at the beginning of the night when the moon is full around the time of witching. Drawing Down the Moon is also an original work that was written by Wiccan Priestess Margot Adler.

Drawing down the sun The same ritual is used for drawing down the moon however, it is used to invoke The Horned God.

Elder: In certain covens, you're considered an elder when you've governed an entire coven over nine years.

Eostara is pronounced with the "e" Silent. Also known as"the Festival of Trees and Lady Day. The festival is observed on Spring Equinox (March 21 in the Northern Hemisphere) and is one of the less popular Wiccan Sabbats.

Esbat is a moon-related ritual that celebrates goddesses and their energies. Twelve esbats occur in the all twelve seasons of the year. Esbat can also refer to an annual meeting of coven. The frequency of the meetings is determined by the coven.

Familiars: Spirits of low rank that take the form of pets that are used by witches to serve as protectors, spies, and as companions. Cats are in witchcraft used for their familiarity, since they are extremely sensitive to psychic frequencies positive energies, negative energy, and have power. This is the reason they are permitted to be part of magical circles. In the medieval era, African witches preferred owls as well as hyenas and baboons. and bats, and European witches favored cats, dogs and toads.

Famtrad: A short form of "family traditions." It's an Wiccan or witchcraft ritual that revolves in the belief system of a single family instead of covens.

Grimoire: A textbook of magic.

Halloween: Also known as Samhain or All Hallows Eve. It celebrates the bounty of the earth, as well as souls of those who have passed away.

Handfasting is a Wiccan wedding ritual.

Hecate Hercules: The goddess of patronage associated with witchcraft from Greek mythology. The goddess is associated with the wisdom of spirits, herbs necromancy, crossroads sorcery, and night.

The Horned God: Cernunnos (Celtic), often referred to in the form of Pan, Zeus, Thor, Adonis, or Hugh. He is depicted as a man goat, or as an object of desire.

Initiation: Rituals to officially welcome an aspiring witch to the coven following Wiccan studies.

Matrifocal: Female-focused.

Pentacle: A symbol of earth. It's a star that has five points with one of them pointed upwards with a circle surrounding it. This makes it distinct against Satan's pentagram. It is the most significant representation of witchcraft. Inverted pentacles with no circles are frequently connected to Satanism or the Church of Satan, and because of this, Wiccans rarely make use of them in rituals to avoid any connection.

Poppets or Puppets: Poppets are made of mud silk, cloth, straw wax, wood, or and bits of hair, nails, skin and even herbs. They are used for various motives like love spells as well as a protection spell or to ward off a curse.

Rules of Three or Threefold Law: A tenet that is followed by Wiccans as well as occultists witches too. It is based on the Law of Karma states:

Never forget that Rules of Three,

Three Times Your Actions Return to Thee.

This lesson is one that you should learn.

Thou only earns what thou Earns.

The Sacred Circle The Sacred Circle is typically nine feet in diameter and created in the air with an athame. The circle is a symbol of cosmic power, and is a symbol of an area between the world with the realms that is the realm of Gods.

Sabbat: Celebration of Earth's orbit through the Sun (the Wheel of the Year) by way of music, poetry and dance. There are eight Sabbat rituals:

* Yule or the Winter Solstice (December 21 - - - N June 21 -- - S).

* Imbolc or Candlemas (February 1 -1 - N, 1 August -S).

* Ostara (Vernal Equinox in March 21,(N, 21 September -(S, N).

* Beltane (April 30 -- N, October 31 -- S).

* Litha (Summer solstice on June 21 -- N, and December 21 -(S, December 21 -).

* Lughnasadh (August 1 -- - N 2 February -- S).

* Mabon (Autumn equinox in September 21 -N, 21 March -- - S).

* Samhain (October 31 (both hemispheres).

Note that N is Northern Hemisphere, and S is Southern Hemisphere.

Scryingis the art of looking at an object (a white mirror, water bowl or crystal ball) to receive images or messages.

Self-Dedication is a personal ceremony in which an witch pledges her self to the Goddess's worship as well as that of her lover who is God of the Horns. God. The ceremony is performed in front of an altar or by a coven by sprinkled with sea salt before lighting candles and then anointing the eyes as well as the mouth, nose belly, breasts and feet with a mix of wine and water.

Wand The symbol of invocation to the spiritual. Wands represent the element of fire and are taken from the branches of trees within sacred forests. The most effective wands are made from trees that are sacred to the goddess including elderberry, mistletoe hazel, rowan, and willow. Wiccans create a pentagram along with their own name on their wands, and then they bless it with the goddess's name. The power of the wand is determined by its witch that holds it.

Witching Hour The Witching Hour is the time of the year when there is plenty of uncertainty about when this occurs the case, but most believe it to fall between 12 AM and 3 AM. This is when the line between our world and the realm of the undead gets thinner and a multitude of unruly creatures are able to cross seamlessly.

The Wiccan Rede is a set moral guidelines for Wiccans. The most well-known is the one that encourages that magic should be used while balancing accountability. It reads:

"Do whatever you want, and it will not harm anyone."

Meaning: so the magic you use doesn't harm anyone else and is not harmful to another, then it's OK.

Many myths about witches.

If you asked someone on the street about what the definition of a witch is and they would probably respond like "bent-nosed women sporting pointed hats, broomsticksand broomsticks boiling hot cauldrons along with spells." It's not hard to blame for them. The depictions of characters such as The Wicked Witch of the West in the movie The Wizard of Oz (1939) or the Grand High Witch in The Witches (1990) don't help. Here are some false myths about witches and the truth about them.

To be a Witch you must be Wiccan. That's not any further than the fact. Your ability to control energy that comes from herbs, plants or rituals, spells or even reading the stars, identifies the witch within you regardless of what religion you belong to. Also, you don't need to belong to a family of witches in order to be one. It's not about purebloods against muggers.

Witches are women, while Warlocks and Wizards are men It isn't gender-specific. Language is a dynamic concept and subject to change. Anyone can call themselves as a witch but no one is able to decide the manner in which witches prefer to be referred to as. Warlock is a derogatory term employed by witches to refer to the male magician who is an outcast, a traitor or one who uses dark or blood magic.

Women and men have practiced magic since as far as we can remember, but women have paid for it in their lives. The notion that witches are female is likely to be a consequence from the reality that the majority of those who were that were accused of and executed for witchcraft were women.

In the Malleus Maleficarum, a Catholic treatise about witchcraft, accused females of being susceptible to the devilish superstitions because of their naturally jealous and a shrewd temperament. This is the reason in many witchcraft practices women are considered to be superior to males.

Witches are Evil, they ride Brooms and eat Babies to stay young The myth of this is a direct result of the first Hollywood films as well as religious fanaticism and pop culture. People can be either good or bad. Also witches can be good or bad. Evil is a natural flaw in character. It is not a result of witchcraft.

Why should we go through the hassle of harming a child with sunscreen and moisturizers that have been developed already? Babies are adorable to all even witches. Witches have children too. But they don't consume salamander tails, or the eyes of young frogs. They cook normal food and go to pizza places and salad bars like everybody else.

Then, let's look at the notion that witches ride Brooms. This is crazy, and here's the reason many people believe it. In the Middle Ages, women made an ointment from ergot an ergot-like fungus that thrived on Rye. They put them in vaginally with Broomsticks. They didn't fly -- at least not physically. They just got high. There's an old story about Pagan rituals of witches that used broomsticks as a simulator to boost the yield of crops.

Witches go around laying curses and Hexes are both spells used to harm people or things. The first causes permanent harm while the latter results in only temporary harm. Magic can be an instrument used by witches to communicate their desires to the world, however the majority of Wiccan practices adhere to the rule of three or the law of three. This means that anything you let into the world will return to you three times over. This helps witches to do their work in a responsible manner and, therefore beware of laying curses.

Being a Witch is expensive It is not necessary to take out your savings or use up all the credit on your card to be an occult. A variety of free Wiccan sources are on the internet. You can also find online covens that you can join at no cost. The tools you need for your altar could be purchased at a dollar shop. If you study further about the subject of witchcraft it is likely that you will realize the "witchy" equipment is everywhere in your home from your kitchen and spice cabinet. If you do have the money on crystals, athames, tools, and such there are online stores that sell them.

All witches wear Black It's the fact that there is no doubt black is an attractive color by itself Many witches enjoy adding a splash of color. They don't have a hat with a pointed tip. There are some who wear sunglasses and fedoras and others prefer black fishnets in black and velvet but others would prefer a t-shirt and comfortable jeans. There are fashion houses too. While witches might be enthralled by this idea owl-delivery option, FedEx and DHL are plenty for them.

Witches worship the Devil and own black Cats First of all, the devil is an Christian idea and does not have anything to do with witchcraft. Certain witches believe in Cernunnos who is known as Cernunnos, the Gaelic Horned God, which Puritans thought was the devil. Witchcraft is not about selling your soul in exchange for magic abilities.

In the case of cats that were black, Druids and Celts were fond of them. They are a symbol of luck and prosperity, love, and security. Since the Christians have launched a crusade against non-Christians cats were portrayed in a negative light. Puritans believed that the cats were witches disguised in the form of animals. At the time of Middle Ages, cats were condemned by Pope Gregory IX and massacred by the Catholic Church. This resulted in an outbreak of rats and then the bubonic plague , also known as "the black death" that was one of the most horrifying plagues in the history of humanity.

Witchcraft is about memorizing ancient Latin verses for spell work Incantations and blessings are a part of the process in witchcraft, however it's not the only requirement to become a fully-fledged witch. The practiced rhymes and poems might be able to assist you attain a higher state or connect with nature forces however the true effectiveness of any spell is not in the words, but rather the strength and clarity of the intent.

To be a real witch It is essential to be a part of a Coven. The word "coven" was popularized in 1921, when Margaret Alice Murray popularized it by using it to describe an assembly of witches. Covens are great if like them, but witchcraft is an individual way. Witchcraft is the path to embracing your power. Find out what you like and then follow your intuition. Are you lucky enough to attend an event that can help you develop as an aspiring witch? Perhaps you'd like to join in which is fine however if you're a solo witch who prefers working on your own, then you can do what you like. This doesn't mean you're a more and lesser witch.

The Lunar Phases and their significance to Witchcraft

Witches are in love moonlight and are able to harness the moon's power to help them with their spells. Witches see that the Sun being male-energy, and moon as feminine energy, or the goddess's energy.

New Moon The moon's primary phase. It is sometimes referred to by the name of crescent moon. It's a lot like an emoji of "D" and the right side of an apostrophe. It is a symbol of a new beginning. The sky usually is dark with the moon hidden. It's the perfect moment to look at our shadows or parts of us that remain in the shadows. Cast spells to assist in getting rid of the old habits, make new plans for the next cycle or let go negative people to allow room for more positive ones.

Waxing Moon The moon increases gradually in size. It is larger than the new moon but not as large like the full moon. It's a great choice for spells that promote growth and progress in your relationships, your career and in just about every aspect of your life. Do you want a fresh job or raise? Perhaps you'd like to bring back the spark in a boring relationship? This is the ideal opportunity to establish your goals.

Full Moon The most powerful period that the moon goes through. The powers of intuition and psychic abilities are elevated and the effectiveness of any spells that are cast during this time is increased by a factor of two. Witches are known in charge of their crystals, or make moon water with this period. Witches can use the full moon's power with sexual magic. A goal set by an orgasm under the light of the full moon will go to be effective.

Waning Moon: Unlike that of the moon in wax, this moon's light diminishes when it transitions back to its night phase. This is a great time to get rid of self-doubt and self-sabotage, unjust treatment, and fears. It is also the time to establish goals to rid yourself of everything you do not would like to see in your life.

Dark Moon Dark Moon not part of the major phase of four, and is often confused with new moon. This phase lasts from one to three days, based on the position of Earth and its distance to the Sun. The moon during this time isn't visible. It encourages the solitude, soul-searching and is a time that blocks you from the things and people you don't want, so you can discover yourself and determine what you value the most.

Middle or Secondary Phases the Moon. Moon

Waning Crescent The crescent moon becomes smaller and less visible until the moon's light disappears.

Waxing Crescent The Waxing Crescent occurs following darkness. It comprises the first third of the waving moon. It has an crescent-shaped sliver of moon, which is less than a half moon.

Waning Gibbous is also known as "the 3rd Quarter. It occurs following when the moon is at its full when the moon's light decreases continuously.

Waxing Gibbous The size of the moon increases to nearly half-full following the crescent's waxing, and the first quarter.

The Best Days to Experience Moon Magic

Even without Moon phases specific days can be energized for specific moon-related magic.

Sunday: In conjunction with the Sun This day is ideal for issues related to fitness and goals, career options agricultural, professional partnerships as well as civic concerns and mental health.

Monday: In connection with the moon Mondays are awash with feminine energy and are the most beneficial days to increase your intuition and understanding as well as regression from past lives spiritual growth, healing medicines cooking skills, and even beauty.

Tuesday: In conjunction with Mars The Tuesday is a day with masculine energy. It is a day to focus on dealing with issues of a more physical nature, such as fitness, sexual and physical endurance, protection rituals and issues that involve law enforcement, and for making new beginnings. It's the perfect day for surgeries, tests and even adopting an animal.

Wednesday: In connection with Mercury. Mercury Wednesday has a connection to concerns of the arts and communication and education, as well as healing, creativity and memory. This is the perfect day to think outside of the box thinking.

Thursday: In conjunction with Jupiter Thursday: Associated with Jupiter, this is the most favorable day for religion and foreign-related pursuits and outdoor activities as well as luck and research, self-improvement as well as spiritual and mental health. The wealth manifestations and competitions in sports are the best of the day today.

Friday is associated with Venus the link between Friday and the goddess in love has symbolic. This makes it the perfect day to experience love, pleasure and fertility, unions and focusing on relationships dating, music and self-expression. The moon's waxing on a Friday is the ideal recipe to conjure romance as well as the best date. There's no surprise that get-togethers and parties take place on the agenda for Fridays.

Saturday Associated with Saturn This is the day for transformation, protection and cleansing of the spiritual. It's also a day to let go of the routines, people, objects and thoughts that are detrimental to you. For instance the moon's waning phase on Saturday is the ideal day to remove a troublesome tenant or guest who has stayed beyond their time.

Chapter 4: Science Of Magic

The world can be very dull and depressing . This is simply the mental state . If, through any practice, we are able to alter the inner reality that is throbbing inside us, then we can alter our destiny and our own life as well .

Life is as if it was a miraculous event . Every second gives us an chance to discover ourselves and transform our lives into an even greater success.

By utilizing the ancient art of meditation, we can broaden our consciousness and discover the more powerful reality that is residing within our own minds . When we look at our dreams with a lot of conviction , have the ability to manifest .

The power of visualization is among the most powerful gift granted to us by God the supreme . Every day, when you wake up each day, try to envision the goals you would like to see the world a better place . It is all feasible in this world of wonder . The question that comes from this is If our world is that amazing, then why have so much suffering in our lives .

It is because we cannot comprehend the essence of our being. Keep meditating on the holy words to discover your real nature.

If you're at peace with your own internal state of consciousness, you are able to manifest everything . It is all possible with an enlightened mind . Therefore, look around look within, explore and discover in all the higher realities inside your . This is the secret method of success within the world .

Our minds are similar to kalpavriksha that is able to offer us any thing . The problem is that we're constantly lost in our thoughts that we're not able to identify the person we truly are. The state of our consciousness is able to do everything in the world . It is the basis of every joy that is present throughout the world .

How do we tap into that potential inside us.

In order to do this, we need to understand what is the essence of our internal energy . It is referred to as kundalini energy, and is composed of four parts . Our mind is the first component that is always busy. Our breath is the second thing that needs to be addressed. falls under the vast discipline of pranayama.

The third element of internalization sexuality .

Therefore, through discipline and deep learning, we need to focus on each of these elements to discover our true self.

The inner world is filled with plenty of potential and power that even without any external achievements it will give us that enormous joy that can make us happy and content within our own world.

The key to success is finding truth and fullness. It's more of a problem of reality inside rather than the external reality.

In each and every day life we are always feeling insecure and weak. There are always elements of human inefficiency . Meditation can help us eliminate the weaker parts of us, and brings new ray of sunshine in our lives.

Chapter 5: The Building Of Your Altar

Since the beginning of the world human beings have had their own areas. There's a room to cook, one to bathe and another one to sleep. It is only natural to have a separate area to worship for a witch who is serious about their work isn't it?

Altars can be large or tiny, a room or a small corner. There is no need for a grand setup or castle with moats and towers that are high. What size is your space will determine if there is an area you can devote to your work. Or you can opt to go "porta-witch," by carrying your altar along. Some people might argue that because God and Goddess dwell throughout all things, every place could be an altar. It's true technically. However being a witch you'd think that your altar should be an area which is more sacred, devoid of negative energies, and dedicated to one specific reason: witchcraft.

Holy Circles Versus Altars

Magic circles, or sacred ones, were utilized in ancient ceremonies as well as Babylonian magic. They are a symbol of non-physical space, like a microcosm, or psychic bubble created using power and purpose. They are intended to protect us from evil forces, and communicating with gods. Holy circles can be drawn by physical means using chalk or salt, rope, sulfur, or ash.

Wiccan circles typically measure nine feet in size but this could change in accordance with the caster's choice as well as the intention of the circle and the available space. Numerous intricate patterns for sacred circles can be found in Grimoires and magical manuals which mostly feature angels as well as others celestial creatures.

An altar is built in the sacred circle. Altars are sacred spaces that are elevated that witches use for spellwork and communicating in communion with Gods. They come in a variety of sizes and shapes. There's no set design that you can choose from. It is possible to make use of an espresso table or a lovely round table from the home improvement section of IKEA. Many people make use of fireplaces, hearths or even the sides of a chimney to create an altar. It is also possible to have an outdoor altar made of an unflattened stone, a tree stump, or an even space with a stang for the center of attention and other artifacts placed around it. In the end, what is a better way to interact with the spirit world than to be in the natural world?

It is important to be cautious when using altars outside. You don't want arrested by police officers while performing an exorcism with an athame in your hand and dressed in a dress and cape. This isn't a particularly attractive image in all honesty. Because of this, some witches prefer altars that are indoors. When designing an altar for your home, it must be constructed from non-conductive substances such as stone, wood silver, brass or gold. Only magical instruments like the athame must be constructed from conductive materials. Most altars designed for purpose are made from willow, which is a tree that is sacred to the goddess. An altar that is square represents the four elements. While an oval one symbolizes the moon, goddess and spirituality.

Altar Location

Traditional witches tend to have altars permanently set in the east or north as their movements are directed to these directions. If they are placed on the northern side, they can bring prosperity and success. If they are in the southern region, they can be excellent for financial and career growth. To the east, it helps to promote health and long-term health. In the West, it increases creativity. It should be placed in the northeast to encourage spirituality and change, the southeast for transformation and partnerships, the northwest for relationships and relationships and the southwest for help. If you're in need of a fresh beginning, the altar should be facing east when the sun rises, since the rising sun signals the beginning of a new day.

If your space isn't able to accommodate such arrangement, you may set up your altar however you'd like, but keep in mind that the place should be a place where you feel secure and secure. If you choose to keep your altar hidden from the eyes of others it is possible to place it in a space with a lock and key, or conceal it so that it appears as if you've got a diverse aesthetic of your interior. Its place of placement is dependent on your mystical desires along with the God or Goddess you revere. If you're looking for the abundance of light, peace and security, placing the altar you place in your dining room or kitchen is recommended. Advice in matters of love or to honor Aphrodite could be placed next to the bathroom vanity or the bedroom. The different cardinal directions are an aspect of our lives.

Cleaning Your space for Your Altar

After you've decided where you want to place your altar then the next step is to tidy your altar both physically and mentally. Physically, wash it using an broom and other cleaning tools. You can invest in the gentle sea-salt-based detergent to accomplish this. Do a psychic cleanse by smudging the area with tobacco, white sage, cedar or sweetgrass. This eliminates psychic debris and helps to re-energize the place to make room for new beginnings. If you want to smudge your altar with all four of the elements I'd recommend these steps:

* A suitable herb The most sought-after are white sage, palo-santo sweetgrass, cedar lemongrass, juniper and lavender. Since the majority of herbs like palo-santo and sage are affected by excessive harvesting, I would recommend that buying ethically-sourced herbs from trustworthy, reliable eco-

friendly stores or websites. The herbs you use to burn represent the earth element and the smoke is a representation of the air.

* A Smudge pot: This is made from metal, ceramic or stone. It symbolizes the element water. It is possible to use an abalone shell to collect the and ash. Be careful not to expose Abalone shells directly to the sun because they may get scorched. You can use a wood stand to keep the pot in place and raise it up to keep the altar from being exposed to direct scorching.

• A source of fire: Lighters matches, lighters, or flint (for the purists).

Feathers and Fans They represent the element of air. The purists prefer feathers from turkeys or painted feathers of eagles. This is not necessary, as you can wrap a yellow ribbon on the smoke stick (yellow can be the colour used to represent air) and move it around , or employ your hands to disperse the smoke.

* Drums and Sacred Drumming : The sounds represents the heartbeat. It is also possible to use pre-recorded drums or shamanic Native American drum music. Do you have no instruments or drums? Don't worry! Pay attention to your heartbeat or create an intention to listen to music, allowing your spirit to complete the task for you.

When smudging, you could be able to say "With this (name of herb) I cleanse my tools and remove any negative energy that is in the area, so that they serve me to my highest benefit" or "Air water, fire earth; purify, eliminate, and dispel."

After you have cleansed your space, allow the herbs to burn out and extinguish them using sea salt or smother the flames by yourself. Begin with a simple prayer like: "I dedicate this space to (name of god). Let it be a place that is filled with joy, encouragement and spiritual development."

To Decorate or not to Decorate?

There is no proper or incorrect items to choose from when creating the sacred area. Many texts define the items that you must place placed on your altar, such as there's a set of rules which outlines what can be placed on your altar and what shouldn't. The book's goal is to alter the story.

One thing to bear in mind is that the choice you make is the most important aspect in regards to your altar. Your altar should express your values and personal preferences. You can store a variety of stuff, or go for a minimalist style, or you can change your decorations according to the seasons or opt for an attractive design on your special day. The choice is yours.

When you build your altar, it is suggested that you create a sense of harmony and balance by putting objects in the place that symbolize the four elements as well as cardinal points.

* A bowl of clear crystals or water symbolizes the west and the element of water.

* A bowl made of salt, earth or a crystal to represent the element of earth and north.

* A few feathers, incense sticks lit as well as a wind chime athame or a fan to represent east and the element of air.

* Incense and lit candles for the fire element and south.

Masks, dolls of cloth crystals, or masks that have old Sumerian symbols of sky, heaven, and spirit.

Include an offering tray with your wishes, such as keys if you want an apartment, or a car figurine if you're looking for cars or coins for an extra source of revenue. The sky is the one that encompasses all other elements using celestial or heavenly symbolism or images.

Make use of gems and crystals as focal points to manifest intentions through your rituals and spells. Be awed by your intuition and avoid rushing when choosing crystals to use for this use.

Choose your crystals based on themes. For instance, Black Tourmaline Obsidian Malachite, Hematite, and Agate are excellent for protecting; Charoite, Celestite, Labradorite, Sugilite, and Angelite enhance psychic abilities. Jade Aventurine Moonstone and Clear Quartz aid in harmony and harmony. Crystals can enhance your goals. When combined with herbs essential oils, or incense, they remove negative energy, enhance your mood, and center you, creating the right atmosphere for magic.

You'll need the Book of Shadows, grimoire or a magic journal. It is here that you will write down your spells and notes recipes, rituals, and spells with your hands. You may also write down the lunar calendar and the corresponding Sabbats. Do not make use of your journal for other purpose that is not important to you. Keep it at the altar should it need to be.

If you'd like you could choose the god or spirit you want to collaborate with. It's completely up to you and is based on the goals you are trying to achieve. For example Lord Ganesh or Goddess Lakshmi and The laughing Buddha are gods associated with prosperity or money spells. They also represent riches. Make an altar in the memory of loved ones who have passed away by putting pictures of food items, objects that they loved on it. A hairbrush or even a cup of coffee prepared according to their preferences would be acceptable, so long as they want it. Make sure that it's safe. If you're working with gods or spirits, you should find offerings that work for them.

Many witches prefer to decorate their altars with the altarcloth. You can purchase one or make it by yourself. Sew or crochet patterns that you feel are meaningful to you. You can even make use of a tablecloth which you could sew runes as well as Reiki symbols if you choose to.

Traditional Wiccan altar cloths are constructed out of natural and sustainable materials such as wool silk, cotton linen, and more. If you have to utilize altar cloths you can color-coordinate them with the intention of the spell. For instance, green represents fertility and abundance. It also represents the Earth mother. Black symbolizes wisdom, protection and self-defense. silver is a symbol of psychic connections, dreams, astral projection and telepathy.

The left-hand side of the altar is usually attributed to the goddess. Set up tools associated to her, such as the pentacle or chalice, cauldron, wands, cauldron crystals, besoms, and a wand. You can also add pictures and figurines depicting the Earth mother If you own them. If they are not available an emerald or silver candle might suffice. In the event that your altar has been dedicated to the Triple Goddess You can make use of three candles to honour her as

Mother (white) Maiden (red) or Crone (black).

The right side of the altar is believed to be God of the Horns. Horned God. Keep items that are associated with him like an athame Book of Shadows, the censer and bolline, as well as the swords here. You could also add a figure or god from his Horned God. If you don't have one and you don't have a gold candle, it may be enough. If you are planning to perform magic, be sure all the tools (candles and pens, journals, candles as well as printed or written ideas such as affirmation words or poetry or poem, oils, herbs lighters and other such items) are set under or on top of the altar. It is possible to include refreshments as ritual sacrifices or to replenish your energy during your work. It is possible to include totems of your favourite and spirit animals, images of your pet, as well as other objects that put you into the zone.

If you must leave the altar's circle by using counter-clockwise movements, make a cut in a doorway using the athame held in your dominant hand and face the northeast. Request a friend to be guarded at the door .

If you're practicing on your own put your broomstick in the entrance to dispel negative energies. After returning do not forget to end the circle with the clockwise direction.

Flower Power for Your Altar

If you're planning to use flowers to decorate your altar, here are some that witches often employ and the significance of them.

* Carnation The word Carnation means strength, healing, luck, energy and protection.

* Daffodil, Tulip, Poppy The meaning of these flowers is fertility in prosperity and love. They also symbolize success, love and luck.

* Daisy, Gardenia, Hyacinth The three are known for their love, flirtation, and protection.

* Geranium, Snapdragon, Lilac: Protection.

* Jasmine Sexuality and seduction.

* Lavender, Rose, Violet: Harmony, peace.

* Lily, Pansy: Happiness, communication.

Your altar, just like your art, is constantly changing. Your goals could change, and you may have to make some adjustments to the objects on the altar in the event of this. What's the worst that could happen? There may be multiple altars to serve different goals. Let the spirit guide you.

Giving Attention to Your Altar

Your altar isn't only holy, it's pulsing with energy that is alive. Would you like to meet someone and then be abandoned on the doorstep or not even noticed? This is why you need to give some attention for your altar as well as "feeding" it helps keep those intentions in check and stops stagnant energy. Here are some tips to take into consideration when looking after your altar:

1. Anoint deities or statues.

2. If there are flowers in your home, you should change them every time you can and then clean the vase to ensure the water remains fresh.

3. Make new candles, then clean off the wax of the old candles.

4. If you're a cool fan, then buy Himalayan salt lamps as well as lamps made of selenite.

5. Lighting candles regularly, and lighting incense that has scents that align with your desire or god.

6. Make sure you sweep the altar area frequently, clean altarcloths, clean up cobwebs, if there are any, and clean statues, in the event that you spray them with oils.

7. Charge your crystals in the glow by the full moon each month.

8. If you have a singing bowl, shake it at least twice per week to increase cosmic energies on the altar.

9. Regularly change offerings. Offerings can be in the form of shells, coins flowers, plants or other things.

10. In your temple, meditate daily or in your chanting, singing dance, or reaffirm the intentions you set on your altar, or make new altars if it is necessary.

11. Thank God and express gratitude. You can bake a cake made with herbs your gods prefer or by saying a simple "thank for your" every time.

Rituals and rituals of the Budding Witch

Rituals are at the core of witchcraft. Rituals are a ritual or ritual that is performed to fulfill the purpose of. Some are formal and have a framework and specific rules, while others are unplanned and governed by instinct. Some of the rituals that are carried out by witches who sit at their altars are:

* Consecration or Hallowing The ritual is performed to sanctify a tool and give it magic powers. It is best done in the waxing or full moon.

* Purification Ritual process assists you in cleansing yourself, your home and the tools you use of everything undesirable and unclean. This is performed prior to performing the magic spell. The initial purification rituals should be done during the night of New Moon.

* Rituals for banishing: They aid in ridding a space or person or instrument of evil entities and stagnant energy. Do them as often as you can.

"Invocation" Rituals They require casting a magic circle to bring the power of a god or higher power within oneself.

* Tracing the Mill Ritual: A traditional ritual used to enhance the spiritual awareness and powers. It involves pacing around using a compass, while keeping your focus at a spiritual focus location, such as the stang or flame.

The witch walks around with her head turned to one side, and then inclined to the back. This blocks certain blood supply to the brain and , in conjunction with the attention being focused on a specific object, creates a trance-like state that is essential to perform magic. The best way to perform this ritual is at an outdoor altar, However there have been witches who were able to "tread the mill" inside.

* Cakes and Ale, or Cakes and Wine Ritual: Serving of drinks to end any ritual. Serve cakes on the pentacle dish as well as wine in a glass or chalice. "Cakes" can be crackers, fruit, cookies or any grain-based dish. "Wine" could refer to ale, juice or water.

Chapter 6: Keeping A Grimoire Or Book Of Shadows

What is the Origin of The Book of Shadows
If modern witchcraft was a real human being and its parents were Gerald Brosseau Gardner and Doreen Edith Valiente. Before meeting Valiente Gardner discovered

fragments of a book he believed was written by the collection that included European witches. He wrote down a number of rituals and practices that were derived from studies of Western and Eastern philosophical esotericism, including Celtic mythology, Tantric yoga Aleister Crowley's work, as well as Enochian wisdom.

Valiente edited and rewritten the material, eliminating some of Crowley's writings but she also added poetry and details of her own. The result was a must-have guide for those who practice Gardnerian Wicca. The original title was not an Book of Shadows. It was referred to as Ye Bok of Ye Art Magical.

The name was changed after Gardner was able to find an issue from The Occult Observer magazine in Brighton, England, containing an article about an ancient Sanskrit manuscript, titled Book of Shadows, written by an Indian palmist Mia Bashir. The article was published in conjunction with High Magic's Aid which is an epic fantasy written by the author. He chose to use the title because it is significant to witches of today.

The Grimoire and Its History

The original definition of a grimoire described it an e-book filled with spells, magic such as invocations, incantations prayers, and a myriad of other methods which were used to summon spirits. Grimoires were used in the past, from early Babylonia, Middle Eastern civilizations as well as in early Renaissance times. Grimoires were associated with any one of the three major world religions--Christianity, Islam, and Judaism--and impacted early science and the arts in Europe and part of Asia. So, no matter how many would not allow their use, these are crucial elements of our culture's history.

Grimoire, also known as "grim-wahr," originates from Middle English "gramere" and Old French "grammaire," which refers to spelling and language rules. The root word is derived from Latin "grammatical" as well as the Greek "grammatikos," meaning: "of letters or grammar." The origins of the word come from the pantheistic era are likely to explain why it's a book which is dedicated to rites of honoring goddesses.

Grimoires used to be illegal. In 1277, the archbishop of Paris demanded the destruction of all texts as well as books and scrolls on demonic conjuration, sorcery and necromancy in 1277. They weren't simply textbooks of spells and magic-related rituals, they were explicitly prohibited. If you were caught with a magical text in the middle ages the penalty was harsh. The punishment was severe until you confessed in the pressure of pain. Following this you were burnt alive by the words on your back, so you didn't forget what brought you to be in problem in the first place.

Regardless of the sacrifices made for these taboo texts, many are willing to die in order to acquire the knowledge contained. This is why fragments of the individual texts and their forgeries have been kept then recreated, circulated over and over.

Magical texts included obscure text and foreign languages, and some with multiple languages. This added to the atmosphere of mystery because the majority of the population were illiterate. The difficulties never stopped people from copying or trying to translate the texts. If these were genuine or not, we'll never be able to know. The only person who could have been there was the one to inquire. If you ask someone, you put yourself at risk of being detained and even torture by the investigators.

Grimoires or grimoires, the way we now know from them, began appearing around the 12th century, the majority of them with unknown and often dead authors. Nobody during the Middle Ages wanted to take credit for the creation of grimoires. They were usually handed out as gifts or "found" from mysterious individuals. The texts of the medieval era had fresh editions created by hand copying older ones, putting themselves at risk.

Grimoires had inspiration from a myriad of sources, and this included but wasn't only

* Jewish angelology and Kabbalistic texts.

* Roman Catholic practices like exorcism rituals.

* Egyptian magical papyri.

The alchemical mystery and the rituals.

* Pagan magical texts taken from Rome, Greece, and the Byzantine Empire.

Famous Ancient Grimoires

From the very beginning, magicians and mystics alike have written about their work.

Some are lost or unaccounted for mostly because the Church viewed them as unclean. There are some that remain and provide some insight into the magical work performed by our ancestors. Below are some of the most well-known grimoires:

1. The Grand Grimoire or Red Dragon The Grand Grimoire or Red Dragon was written in French about the middle of the 17th century It is a work of demonic conjuring, necromancy and one of the most evil texts ever composed. The demon summoned is Lucifuge Rofocale. He is an elusive demon. The summoning of this demon is only recommended when you have the chance of entering into a contract with it. The legend says that it will claim the soul of a person after twenty years faithful service.

2. The great Albert written by Albert Magnus: The full title of the Grimoire is: Albertus Magnus, being the Approved and Verified Natural and Sympathetic Egyptian Secrets or White and Black Art for Man and Beast The Secret Knowledge and Secrets from Ancient Philosophers. The first German manuscript was composed in 1478. It's a

book about mysticism and medicine, with solid Christian roots.

3. Grimoire from Honorius the Great Written in the name of Pope Honorius III prior to his demise in the 1227 year This is a magical text that has Christian principles, intended meant for Christian sorcerers. It includes spells for summoning, dispelling or commanding demons, along with animals sacrifices and prayers and directions on how to make the perfect book.

4. Clavicula Salomonis (Keys of Solomon) and the Lemegeton (Lesser Key of Solomon): These texts influenced the grimoires of all time. These were written in Greek by King Solomon who was the most powerful mystic of the world and is it is believed that they existed alongside fragments discovered in the 4th century. The oldest copy that is still in existence is at the British Museum and contains ancient ritual Jewish magic that can influence the spirits and call them to their homes. The book also contains rituals for animal sacrifice. In addition, the Grand Grimoire contains some information from the Clavicula Salomonis.

5. Munich Manual of Demonic Magic (15th Century) Also known as Liber Incantationum, Exorcismorum et Fascinationum, it was written in Latin and includes Roman Catholic rituals for invisibility as well as summoning and banishing demons through sacred circles and powerful words.

6. Picatrix (Ghayat al-Hakim -The Objective of the Wise): Written in Arabic in Andalusia by the mathematician al-Majriti, who lived in 1000 CE, when Spain had been under Islamic rule. It is a collection of four books on astral, talismanic and magical empathy, rooted in the classical Arabian magic, with a reference to Hermes Trismegistus. It includes spells to heal and love, as well as longevity as well as control over and escape from the wrath of enemies. The most extensive and rarest grimoire ever made It has been translated in Latin to serve the king Alfonso the Wise in 1256.

7. The sacred book of Abra-Melin, the Mage It is one of the most complete and powerful magical grimoires. It is described by Crowley as the most powerful and most dangerous work to be found, the book was composed

in 1458, written by Abraham from Worms to the son of his Lamech. Abraham learned the wisdom through the Egyptian magician and Kabbalah master, Abra-Melin. Twelve manuscripts are available with each in the language of a different.

8. The Sixth and Seventh Books of Moses: These controversial texts include incantations to summon, banish and the spirits of command. The later texts are filled with secret concerns about Vatican and Jewish conspiracy theories. It is believed that the text was that it was revealed to Moses at Mount Sinai, then passed through generations until King Solomon utilized it to summon spirits, the book was written using a mixture of Hebrew, Latin, and German. The sixth book is filled with magic seals, as well as the seventh book, magic tables.

9. The Leland's Grimoire or Aradia The Gospel of the Witches: American folklorist Charles Godfrey wrote this at the close in the late 19th century. It was among the first English grimoires to be heavily influenced by neo-Paganism and Wicca The Grimoire is a source of magic lore told by an unknown witch called Maddalena who is believed to

have received wisdom via an older group of Goddess worshippers.

A lot of historical grimoires can be found in private collections as well as national museums such as The Arsenal Library (Paris) and the British Museum (London), with some costly (albeit doubtful) books that claim to be the originals, and occasionally appearing available for sale at auctions around the world as well as online.

Grimoires with different types

Spell Books: A book of spells that includes directions, ingredients, and illustrations of spells either written or discovered.

Journals are invaluable for young witches. A book with a broad range of content that includes a history about your belief system, the journey as a witch, the progress made, the obstacles as well as your own thoughts. They are composed in non-structured format.

Pocket Grimoire Portable notebook that contains basic and emergency magick, herb, components crystals, ideas, and other ingredients that come to mind on the way.

Dream Book: Similar in design to the journal It's a record that includes dreams, astral journeys, symbols, interpretation of dreams and even projections out of body.

Grimoires that are subject-specific: They come in a variety of dimensions, styles and subject categories based on the type of witchcraft used or researched. You can find grimoires for runes, tarots and sigils, herbal or the study of astrology.

Religious Grimoire: It is used to document your faith. It could also include prayers, devotional practices or holy day celebrations.

Montage Grimoire: A general-purpose grimoire. This is the complete record of your practice. This is the time difficult to categorize your work into categories.

Questions to ask yourself prior to beginning a Book of Shadows/Grimoire

1. What is your opinion on size? Would you rather a compact text, or one you bring out for special events?

2. Do you plan to write daily entries? Do you prefer to make entries on specific occasions

, like casting on sabbat, or even during new or full moons?

3. What do your entries appear like? Would you like to create to create an instructional manual? Do you wish to include your thoughts or even your dreams?

4. What is the role you see the book taking on? It could be a reference or an advisor? What are your goals with it?

5. Do you need a private draft, or would you rather a manuscript that you can write in with your partner or other coven members?

6. Where would you store your book? What about your altar, in a safe deposit box or an indoor safe or maybe a hole in the floorboards?

7. Would you create the book by yourself, buy one, or even go digital?

8. What would you like to happen to your personal book in case of passing? Do you wish to have it passed down, handed over to anotherperson, or deleted?

Answering these queries can assist you when creating, storing and how to structure your book. There are no two grimoires or Books of Shadows can be identical even if they were written by twins. To make it truly yours, you can add images, zodiac symbols pictures of gods or botanicals, your personal animal, tarot cards or even the eye of Horus Anything is acceptable. It's yours to write.

Criteria for Inclusion

There isn't a hard and fast rule on what the content of your book must be. However, there are universal elements.

Traditions or laws of the Coven: Principles differ from one group to another Therefore it is recommended to record these practices at the very beginning of the book. If you're being an eclectic witch, or a part of a religion that has no defined rules, you may want to make a list of the appropriate rules to practice magic. The best examples are the Three-fold law as well as Wiccan Rede. Wiccan Rede.

Dedication: If involved in a coven you may write down an in-depth account of the ceremony you attended for your initiation. Self-dedications to gods can be written down, as well as the reasons why God has been chosen. The writing you write about can be a short paragraph or an essay. One example would be "I (name) commit myself to serving the Triple Goddess this day, on 20 February 2020."

Choose Your Deity: This is contingent on the pantheon you select. You can be monotheistic (one God)) as well as polytheistic (many gods). If you're a collector of spiritual paths that are different or myths about a god you cherish and keep track of the celestial influence by recording them.

Correspondence Tables: All spellcasters acknowledge the importance of correspondence tables as essential tools. They include crystal and herb pictures lunar phases, their functions. For the entire year Tables can be traced using the Wiccan almanac. It includes lunar phases, the dates, and information about herbs that can be consumed.

It's the Wheel of the Year: It includes eight holidays for witches. Included are rituals, esbats and sabbats and rites of honoring your family's ancestors. You may choose to follow a an established routine or switch the rituals with each holiday. Include notes on casting circles, healing for the home, house or prosperity blessings, and also the moon's descent to honor the goddess of motherhood.

Divination: It includes types of divination such as scrying, astrology gazing or palmistry. Keep track of everything you have learned and the experiences you have with divination for yourself and other people.

Magical Texts: In addition to your Pagan or Wiccan texts that you have at your disposal, add details from manuscripts that appeal to you, for instance To Ride a Silver Broomstick or The Spiral Dance. Prayers and old invocations in old languages are also welcome.

Kitchen Witchery: A lot of witches will be making something or another in their kitchens. While you are developing recipe ideas for your spells recipes for food for oils, sabbat as well as herbal mixtures make sure to keep the recipes in your book. Alongside having them on hand whenever you require them, it's an enjoyable present for those in your family that may be curious about witchcraft.

Spellwork The spell work is optional. You can write your spells into separate books (grimoire) or in your Book of Shadows. If you store your spells as well as other subjects in a single volume it is best to arrange them, particularly in the case of unique. Be sure to make room to document the duration of casting, results as well as the casting partners (if there were any) and any adjustments.

Keeping a Grimoire

The Book of Shadows is a book that contains magical rituals, practices or traditions, as well as whatever you want to record about your magical experience. Wiccan traditionalists favor handwritten books, however the advancement modern technology has rendered the concept obsolete. There's no one method to create these books, therefore choose the method that works for you. This is a sacred document that deserves to be blessed by your magic tools. If the content is written in hand ensure that they are written in a clear and legible manner. This makes it easy to read or remember the rituals.

The Art of Organizing Your Book of Shadows (BOS)

You can create your own BOS by yourself or purchase one from the retailer or online.

Three-ring binders are the best choice to permit recipes written down to be entered or altered as required. This way it is possible to use sheet protectors to keep the drippings of candle wax, ritual drippings and ink from leaking onto and staining your page.

Include your name as a crafter in standard letters or scripts, with the title of your book on the front page. Spells must be legible. If you decide to write in simple English or some other type of lettering ensure that it's easy to read.

The most difficult part is organizing it. There are a myriad of resources available including a table contents at the start or a comprehensive index in the back. A continuous study will help you decide on what to include and which you should eliminate. Take note of the information in the magical books that you've read and information sources. This will make it easier when you must communicate information to others. Ringed binders make sharing and exclusion much easier.

Many witches have separate books for their original designs and the other for data downloaded from the Internet. Grimoires digitally stored should be secure and kept on compact disks, flash drives or even on cloud storage for convenient online access. One stored on a hard disk is just as valid as the one written by hand on parchment.

Tips for Book Organization Tips for Your Book

Start your grimoire by introducing poetry, a blessing or inspiring quote: it's more memorable when it's something you created by yourself. Invoke the Goddess for protection and guidance. Make sure you write with intention, since every entry in your journal is a ritual of magic by itself. You can use an entirely different poem or blessing for each entry, or the same for all entries.

Spell Sorting: Make separate columns or pages for regular spells as well as special occasion spells. For example cleansing rituals and protection and healing spells can be included in the normal category, during sabbats or handfasting ceremonies in the category of special occasions.

Arrange according to Topic: If organizing according to categories proves an issue, you can create a table of contents to categorize spells according to the topic or their purpose. Sections for protection may include black indexes and love sections could contain pink indexes and areas of abundance could be green.

Sort by Component: This type of arrangement arranges spells according to the ingredients they contain. Make sure to organize your book with distinct sections for candles poultices for herbal remedies crystal magic, crystal poultices and more. By sorting them this way, you can see in a glance which magick to do with the ingredients available.

Date Every Entry The idea of a date may seem unimportant and yet, without dates how do you know the amount of time between the time the spell was cast, and the time it was manifested? In addition dates place your thoughts and experiences into an environment that allows you to understand the spiritual journey you've been on over the years.

Record the spell work When you cast the spell, take note of the spell down. Include any relevant details such as the purpose of the spell, in the event that the spell was for personal use or on behalf of anotherperson, the place the spell was cast, if there was anyone involved, what spell-working tools employed, as well as the steps to follow.

The Digital BOS

If you're a tech-savvy person and like having your BOS mobile You might want to think about a digital version. There are numerous applications that you can utilize when you go down this method. A tablet, phone or laptop is sufficient for an easy and editable Book of Shadows. Plus, it can fit into your purse, pocket or bag. Google Keep Notes, Microsoft OneNote or DraftPad assist in creating basic folders and files.

Do you need a digital magical journal? Consider apps such as SomNote, Diaro, and Journey. Its Gilded digital Book of Shadows is a complete app that includes 40plus digital stickers, spellwork templates and four cover pages in addition to other options.

Secure and upload notes to your grimoire with ByWord, SimpleNote, and iAWriter. These programs allow you to access, store and print files easily across various devices.

When you upgrade to the latest software, make sure you convert your files to the latest format that allows for quick access. And don't forget to make backups of everything!

Crafting Your Grimoire

Grimoires of the past are written in papyrus parchment, or even paper. Bindings were constructed of intricately decorated wood, velvet, or another tapestry that was richly torn leather or engraved metal dependent on the materials the author could acquire. Rich witches and occultists adorned theirs with gems and gold leaf.

Witches of modest origin decorated their houses with dried flowers, and carved magic on stone and pieces of bark from trees. If you're one of the witches who are "going environmentally friendly," then consider recycling old papers to create your own.

If the cover of your book is made of cloth make pockets to keep gems, herbs or other small, items that are magical. The covers of soft materials can be equipped with holes in order to create bindings with natural materials such as vines, twine or ribbons. Make sure to use only the finest paper so that your ink won't run. Grimoire pages must are flat and do not move around, disrupting the flow of your work. If the volume is huge purchase a book stand to make sure that your book doesn't take up a lot of space on your altar.

The difference between the BOS and a Grimoire

The majority of Wiccans have an BOS but not a grimoire. Some keep both, and some choose to keep neither as the matter of personal preference. The problem is "What's different between the two?" Think of a BOS as a diary of a witch. It contains a record of your the experiences, rituals, discussions with spirits from other realms, findings about how to follow the goddess's path, fantasies and other important information and personal preference. It's where you can express your creative ideas without fear of criticism or the fear of being judged. It can also include magickal work or random actions to keep track of your spiritual progress. In this way, you will be able to determine the things that work and what isn't working.

Grimoires are the same as BOS, but it is not as personal. BOS however the latter isn't as personal. Grimoires are like a witch's book or manual. If you were to have an old journal as well as a textbook or manual you would know which one belongs on your bedside table and which one would go to the shelves. Grimoires contain spells, rites and potions and instructions on how to prepare, handle and care for magical tools. It also contains a comprehensive list of correspondences and magical tables moon phases herbs, crystals foods recipes, colors and research. There are no personal thoughts or documents of spells cast who, when, how and in what order. As a beginner witch you may want to keep a notebook that serves as a magical journal and an encyclopedia of rituals as well as spells.

As your beliefs, spirit and your craft develop You could decide to take some time to make two distinct books. This will allow you to communicate your research to others without having to reveal your personal thoughts. The books should be blessed and treated with careful handling. A grimoire could be placed on your altar, or placed in an elfin or drawer for easy access, whereas books of shadows ought to be stored in a safe place and out of the reach of prying eyes as it's a very private book.

If you own both books, you can put it in an undiscovered location that you prefer. If you decide to reveal you BOS to anyone else, it must be someone that you can trust and who won't harm you or your book's contents by divulging the contents, handling the book with care or making marks on it without permission.

Finally, every grimoire is one of the Book of Shadows, but not every Book of Shadows is a grimoire. I believe that the information you put in the contents of your BOS or grimoire must be as distinctive in the same way as your. For those who are adamant about it, grimoires must be useful, informative filled with information, annotations, and practical applications. They say that thoughts should are not appropriate for an article. However, as a witch you have to agree that it's hard to say the least, and it is nearly impossible to separate your thoughts as well as your thoughts and work. They all form part of your personality. Remember, you're human and not a closet.

BOS/Grimoire Security

The Book of Shadows or grimoire could be your own creation however, some ethical concerns are present. Note this, especially if are new to the world of witchcraft.

1. As per keeping with Wiccan practice of secrecy don't list the actual names, telephone numbers, addresses for houses or email addresses of other Wiccans and coveners. The book could contain initials, pseudonyms or even craft names However, make sure they can't be traced back to legitimate names or contact numbers.

2. Be cautious about publishing your work with cattlemen. Even if your exuberant it is not a good idea to hurt the confidences of the other actors listed within your work. A special caution must be taken in online or digital versions in your BOS.

3. Do not play with another witch's book without their permission. Many witches believe these books have a personal power, which could be altered or disturbed you

come in contact with someone else's energy.

4. If your book contains rituals or spells that aren't original Don't forget to mention the author's or caster's name. If not, make sure to declare that the work is not yours.

5. If you have to swear specific information, write down the vows in your books. In the event that you forget, you could regret it the vows later.

6. Include instructions on how your book will be dealt with upon your death. A lot of covens and old tradition require that the book be destroyed or handed over to coveners who are in similar situations. No matter if you're single or a member of covens, you should protect your legacy by making sure that you have someone who is trustworthy to take charge of it.

7. Apply a spell of protection to your BOS to ensure security. The grotto and the grove pentacle, the grove, along with the Celtic knot are excellent examples of Wiccan protection symbols. If you're extremely secure, put an inscription on the page of your book or purchase one made that way. Consider investing in a drawstring bag and

silk wrapping to shield it from the effects of ambient energy or dust mites.

8. You can add all or just a few entries in your book with code, so that the details contained remain private. In this way, if anyone happens to discover the book's contents they will not be able to translate them effortlessly. You could try some ancient scripts including Theban, Pictish, Ogam Bethluisnion, Egyptian hieroglyphics, Germanic/Danish/Swedish or Norse/Scandinavian/Seax Wiccan runes, Malachim, Angelic, or Passing the river.

Chapter 7: Breaking The Code Of Divination

Psychic Powers

It's awe-inspiring that divination has endured throughout time, particularly with it being the Catholic Church's vision of the world during the Middle Ages. There was little in the way of entertainment, and so divination as well as other forms such as "heresy" were punished with humiliation in public and even beheading (at the very least) or even being cooked alive.

It's fun for cynics and religious scholars due to the fact that the Church in some parts of Britain and Europe in the past was a believer in Bibliomancy as a method of divination based on the Bible. Many believers believed that opening it randomly could provide answers to their questions and also gave predictions. Children with insomnia were given the Bible (a grimoire for the religious If we're honest) put over their heads. The pregnant women were read the Bible to ensure safe delivery. Witchcraft-related accusations were assessed on the basis of the Bible then, in the event of being they were found lacking, they were executed. But I digress. This chapter isn't all about the battle between grimoires.

Divination has its roots into the Middle English word "divinare," which means, "to predict." It's an opportunity for the person who is interested in learning and tap into the collective unconscious mind. It allows you to be aware of past, present and the future. A lot of witches use some kind of divination, and provide crucial psychological and spiritual advice when they have to make crucial choices in their lives.

Man hasn't even begun to get close to the variety of methods for divination are available. In the past, in Babylon priests believed in the haruspic sound, which resembles the sound of a dish, but is actually divination using animal entrails , or oil drops placed in a basin. This chapter will discuss the most popular divination methods that exist , as well as some myths surrounding the divination methods.

Selecting an System

There are a myriad of different systems that are available, each having books devoted to their study. It is yours. If you're looking to add divination to your practice, I would suggest that you do not spend any money on it until you're certain it will appeal to you. Do not become a system junkie.

Test tools are available. If you're using Tarot, for instance, you can ask the same question but in different ways to test the consistency of your responses. Record them in your BOS so that you can keep track of their efficacy. Select a method of divination that resonates with you, gives you clear and precise messages and is easy to master.

Know that the outcomes or results from any method don't indicate that your destiny (or that of someone else) is fixed. The future doesn't have to be set in the stone. Explore the designs and systems that are part of your past and your the culture. I suggest this since you're likely already familiar with its significance. If a god from one particular culture, such as that of the Mayan It-Zamn, or Celtic Morrigan, fascinates you it is possible to select a religion from these sources.

Popular forms of Divination

The Pendulum Dowsing method: Ancient Greeks and Romans utilized this to determine the future. It's the most straightforward form of divination that you can learn since it only gives a yes or no or possibly. This method is a great way to locate lost pets and objects, detect allergies, determine your goal, identify negative energies, locate water lines or ley lines and much more. It functions by transmitting energy through intuition, and decoding messages from angels, guardians and others spiritual guides. Pendulums of all kinds are readily available. There's no need to purchase the most expensive one to achieve excellent results. A lot of people utilize things as basic as a string or a key suspended from string.

Make it using a gemstone or crystal that is wrapped in jewelers wire, and a lighter chain of between ten and 14 inches. You can also opt for one made from clear quartz, which helps to improve your mental clarity and a connection to a greater reason. Rose quartz and amethyst are both good choices. You can also have multiple pendulums. Be sure to clean and charge them following use. Wrap them in silk or store in drawstring bags for security.

Tasseomancy It is derived in the French term "tasse," meaning cup and Greek "mancy," meaning "to divine." Tasseomancy involves interpreting patterns found in Tealeaves, wines or grounds of coffee. It is a tradition that originated in Asia and in the Middle East, and Ancient Greece.

Chinese at the time of the 2nd millennium B.C.E. began divining with loose tealeaves that left patterns on the bottom of cups. The modern tasseography was developed in the 17th century , after trading routes introduced tea into Europe through China. When tea consumption increased across Europe as did the practice of tasseomancy. Crescent moons symbolize the fame of the world, elephants symbolize good health birds are good luck and triangulars bring bring good luck.

Numerology: It's divination based on numbers. It's based on the notion that every number has a distinct energy signature that provides insight into one's personality and future. Certain numbers have more power in comparison to other numbers. The three main versions that make up this method are Qabbalic, Chaldean, and Pythagorean. A combination of each of them can be utilized in a reading. However, it's better to use just the same one in order to avoid confusion results.

Kabbalistic numerology comes from Jewish mysticism. This is the Hebrew alphabet as well as its 22 vibrations are utilized to interpret names. Chaldean numerology was first discovered in Mesopotamia where it was the origin of Western Astrology. It is tightly linked to planetary relationships. It is in this way that the single numbers represent your exterior character, while double numbers reveal your inner characteristics.

Pythagoras invented Pythagorean numerology during the sixth century. He used it to forecast individual fates as well as the fate of certain locations. He even went further to alter the future of people by altering their names.

In the modern world of numerology, your path to success will be the product of all the numbers that you have in your birth date reduced down to one digit, ranging between one and nine. It is not the case when they are added to master numbers like 11 or twenty-two. The number that determines your destiny is the total of your name as it appears on the birth certificate. The total number of consonants within your name reveal your personality number, while the vowels make up your soul's number.

Rune Casting Runic Alphabet (Futhark) is an alphabetic system of writing created by the Germanic people in Scandinavia, Iceland, Northern Europe as well as Britain in the 3rd century. Legend says that Futhark came to be discovered by Odin when he was hanging on the branch in Yggdrasil during nine consecutive days. Futhark contains twenty-four letters.

Rune is one of the Proto-Germanic word that translates to "mystery" also known as "secret." When translated into Finnish it translates to "poem," and in Lithuanian, "to speak." In older English the word "ridan" signified "interpreting runes" as "writan" signified "carving ranes." It's possible that these could be the words that were re-interpreted to be used in contemporary English in the form of "read" as well as "write." Runic letters were found on weapons and jewelry dating to the 3rd century. Futhark is much more than letters. It is a symbol of the cosmic forces that govern the universe as well as the Gods themselves.

Running is the process that makes use of runes that are laid out in a particular pattern or randomly to help you with the process of problem solving and decision making. It's like magical scrabble. There is no standard method for casting, but the most common designs are three-rune and the nine-rune cast. Runes are made from various materialslike clay, crystals, bone wood, metal, or wood. You can buy them or make your own.

The concept of rune-casting is that it concentrates on both the subconscious and conscious minds simultaneously. Do not expect precise answers such as when you'll get married or die or be millionaire. Don't expect concrete advice either. Runes are only able to provide some suggestions or potential outcomes in light of the current situation. The answers given do not come from a random source. Your subconscious is the source of these answers. Utilize runes whenever you need clarity about an issue or you are unable to see the complete view.

I Ching or Yi Jing or Book of Changes: This is an old Chinese oracular text that was used in the field of cleromancy (casting lot). The system was developed in China to help answer all of life's issues. The first method involved throwing fifty yarrow sticks. But as time passed the use of coins was introduced. I Ching uses six random numbers between 6 and 9, placed within the King Wen sequence--a hexagram of six lines, which is formed by coins or reeds.

Hexagram lines can provide predictions for the future and past. This method that is used to determine the future is founded on concept of five elements:

* Huo (fire).
* Jin (metal).
* Shui (water).
* Tu (Earth).
*Mu (wood).

They form the basis of everything else that exists within the Universe. I Ching is also founded upon the notion that of Yin and Yang, which is the concept of dualalism and the interconnectedness of everything and Bagua cosmic permutations that reveal the basic realities of reality, as represented in eight trigrams as well as sixty-four Hexagrams.

In this type of divination the three coins are tossed around six times (for Hexagram lines). The patterns are created as they fall on the right spot, and they provide answers to specific questions. I Ching is unique because it doesn't give you precise explanations. It simply helps you discover the answers in your own mind. It doesn't matter what you throw the issue is your perspective because your concentration is required to discern the results in your mind's subconscious.

Chiromancy or palmistry: Studying the hands is the way this method of divination is achieved. The palmist looks at the lines of the palm along with hand's shape and size in relation to the length of your fingers. There is a lot you can learn about someone's mental, physical and emotional state through their hands. The details about their past future, and present can be discovered.

Palmistry has been practiced for more than 3000 years. It became widespread during the Zhou dynasty. Different versions of this art are found in many different cultures The most well-known are the ones taught in Vedic Astrology, Romani culture, and Chinese practices.

The left-hand displays innate traits and accounts for 20% of readings, whereas the right hand displays postnatal information, which accounts for the majority of readings. Since your hands are always changing, what you read two years ago could differ from a more recent reading. These are the most important lines that matter , and what they symbolize:

*Heart line Love, passion and love.

* Headline"Wisdom and intelligence.

* Life line: Vitality symptoms of illness that can occur.

* Fate line: Career, destiny.

Since its beginning the practice of palmistry has been a highly regarded psychic science. Great leaders such as Alexander the Great picked soldiers for commanding troops on the basis of their readings of their palms.

Islam, Christianity, and scientists have dismissed this as "hocus-pocus." However, no matter the way you slice it the hand is an absolute masterpiece. Science has also agreed. This is why there's an entire field of research of fingerprints and hand, Dactylography. Dusting off fingerprints is the essential part of every crime scene. What further evidence do you need to convince yourself that your hands are holding the power?

Scrying: The word "scrying" comes from an ancient English phrase, "descry," meaning, "to make out dimly." This is where you look at reflective, refractive luminescent, or transparent surface to observe images that show things that happen. The surfaces include crystal balls, clouds, water reflective obsidian polished, mirrors or glowing candles, polished stones as well as eggs, fishing hooks, or polished and polished materials. Many prefer to look at their inner eyes, a practice known as eyelid scrying.

It isn't just associated with Gypsies. Different cultures use it. Egyptians utilized the ink to paint water. The Egyptian goddess Hathor had a shield which was able to reflect all things in their real nature. This shield is the reason that the first magic mirror was created. In the past, Persian writings from the tenth century referred to of the Cup of Jamshid used by the occultists to study each of seven levels in the Universe.

Ancient Celts, Aztecs, and Greeks written using black glass, beryl polished quartz, crystal and water. Nostradamus was one of them. He predicted using a bowl of water set on the tripod of brass. Mesopotamians employed oil-filled bowls. In the past, Arabs employed polished thumbnails. John Dee, personal magician to Queen Elizabeth I, employed polished obsidian as well as a tiny crystal egg, which is currently kept at the British Museum, London.

Mirrors and other reflective surfaces can be gateways for the spirits world permitting messages and messages from loved family members and other spirits to be transmitted through the highly reflective surface. Witches and shamans typically covered their scrying tools in black clothing when they weren't being used to keep these "doorways" shut.

Tarot: This is a form of cartomancy--predicting the future, understanding the present, and gaining insight into the past using cards. Tarot decks are comprised of seventy-eight card comprised of four suits with 14 cards each (ten numbers cards along with four court cards) known as the minor arcana, as well as 22 trump cards, referred to as the arcana major. Arcana is Latin meaning "mysteries" which translates to "secrets." Tarots help in self-understanding, understanding and prediction, as well as guidance and healing.

There is no consensus on the source of the Tarot. Tarot experts and occultists such as Eliphas Levi, and Etteilla believe they are derived from the past of Egypt. Others believe that it's an ancient Chinese invention. There's no evidence to back either of these theories. The theory that appears more likely is that Romani introduced tarot to Europe. While the exact date is not known these cards were in use since the 14th century.

Every tarot card has a symbolic significance. The major arcana is a symbol of life-altering choices, beginning with foolish (0) and concluding by the end of the world (XXI). They depict your physical and spiritual journey through life. After that, you pass away and reincarnate starting from zero. Minor arcana includes pentacles, swords, cups and wands. Court cards are kings page, queen, and king (or princess in certain decks).

They show your personality and your individual perception of situations and the others. Numerological cards depict the different events, beginning with the ace and concluding with the tenth card. Each card is upright and reversed version. You can take a look on both sides or turn the card upside down.

The most popular Deck is called the Rider-Waite which is a popular most popular choice for both beginners and professionals alike. Many believe that your primary deck is given to you. This is a common belief because you cannot make a choice by gift cards. It's much more satisfying to select the deck that appeals to you. Do you like the old-fashioned decks or the modern ones? There is no deck that is better than another, so make note of your emotions while you look around on your computer or off.

Divination Spells

Temperance Spell of Scrying

You'll need a lake or a body of water inside the form of a chalice and a temperance card.

Then, take a look at your Temperance as well as the Angel Card (XIV). It will help you get into the right mindset to be able to scry. Concentrate on it with an open heart, believing that you will get the correct information. Allow it to infuse your life with its power.

Chant:

"Temperance card" and water still

Increase my vision, grant my desire.

Be honest, so you can gain knowledge,

and images dance through the reflection plane."

Meditation: Concentrate on your reflective surface that is, the water. Be aware of the exchange of energy between the card and water. Imagine this as white light going between your card and water. The process will improve your ability to scry , and increases the endurance levels of your body. Then, project the card over the surface of scrying within your mind's eyes and feel the energy flowing through your body. Be grateful to the angel for the guidance it provides and keep your eyes fixed on the reflective surface. The energy will flow freely through the waters and your. Keep it the same way until you've got a clear vision.

Right Decision Spell

To perform this spell, you'll require to have the Two of Pentacles and the Hanged Man cards.

This spell can be used for direction, particularly if you are in a bind. Make sure it is completed at least twenty-four hours prior to your decision. It's the Two of Pentacles symbolizes the equilibrium between options and the Hanged Man symbolizes one who is caught in a web of uncertainty.

Then, you must place the Hanged Man in front of you. He represents the intersection. Get rid of the Hang Man's clutches. the failure to take an informed decision is a choice too.

Then, put then the Two of Pentacles before you. Take a look at the options available to you.

Chant:

"Resolutions or resolutions are all there.

Let me see the larger picture. I will never be a victim.

Securely secured, I'll be.

Select the one that is most suitable to me."

Take the decision you need to take in your head until one strikes you as the best choice. Think about the advantages and cons of your decision for 24 hours prior to formally revealing it.

Chapter 8: The In Vocational Power Of Invocation

Since the beginning of time, people have been fascinated and sensitive to the world beyond our own. While it is invisible to our eyes yet it impacts us every day. Our ancestors had knowledge of these realms and made animals and other objects to control and represent them.

The spirit realms, the astral, planetary, the elemental and celestial all contain entities that are passively communicating with you on your physical world. The goal of an occultist, witch or Wiccan is to be able to stay alert to these realms, to intuitively detect their messages, and connect with the spirits of these worlds. One of the methods used to communicate with the spirits of other worlds actively is to invoke.

What's the meaning of an invocation?

Invocation is the act of inviting a god or spirit presence to exercise their power or to fulfill a wish. It is a form of conjuration. Invocation utilizes the spiritual qualities of holy words sounds and names to achieve harmony and alignment with the entities' minds. Invocations are crafted with extreme attention because they are prone to be a disaster. To draw the attention of an individual power or spirit, the person making the request must acknowledge their characteristics strength, qualities, and virtue Therefore, total respect is provided.

Invocations are governed by one rule They must be spoken loudly and not considered in silence. All senses and faculties must be engaged in the invocation. The most intense and powerful vibrations feasible must accompany the invocation as invocations are to imbue oneself with prayer.

In magic, the invocations are performed during the casting of sacred circles to call for the presence of certain spirits that will witness and offer protection during rituals. Invocations are also used to facilitate temporary possession as is seen when performing mediumship or trance ceremonies as well as channeling. The most frequently requested applications of invocation are:

* Healing.
* Wealth generation.

* Discovering love.

* Protection from enemy attacks, evil eyes as well as bad luck.

* Higher chance of conception.

Grimoires and other books of magic have a wealth of ritualistic instruction and invocations. Orthodox Christianity also has rites which involve invocations of their god which is, in this instance, God. For instance, the Lord's Prayer, for instance is a very popular prayer. Pagans and occultists also invoke gods too. However, the only distinction is the rites do not have to be only limited to a single God however, they can also be invoked by other Gods of various pantheons depending on the goals they are designed for.

Another distinction among Christian invokers and the ones performed by those who practice the occult is that the occultists take one step further than benedictions or the Eucharist. They either merge with the deity invoked or alter the power of the gods invoked, applying these power to a sacred weapon, amulet or talisman.

Motives for Invocation

1. To merge with God, you must speak and act in the way it is, and act like an oracle. This is the case in African Voodoo, and invocation is displayed through an elaborate ritual of ecstatic dance.

2. To bestow blessings to one's self or to bestow upon them the power. For instance, the placing of hands at the time of initiation confers the power.

3. To direct, as an entity would have it, the spirits that are under his control will assist the invoker. For instance, a call to Lucifuge Rofocale could trigger demons that are under his control such as Marbas, Bael, and Agares to be invoked. When you call Thoth as the Egyptian god of writing, wisdom and the moon you may trigger an effective invoke of Hermes or the Greek version of Thoth or Mercury Thoth's Roman counterpart.

4. The intention is to allow the person to understand the essence and power of the god, this energy can be utilized to power an amulet, or talisman, and remain efficient even after the ritual has ended.

5. The ability to alter the power of a god or force, in the same manner as elements to charge elementsal weapons.

A good example of an Invocation that calls for the Four Quarters in the Ritual

"I call the Lord and lady fair

I am calling to me the air element.

I appeal to the ancients for wisdom from long ago,

To be present in this evening and to keep my heart in place.

Lord and Lady protect me, protect me from danger

The element of air trust me with a touch of charm.

Oh, the old ones I beg you to favor me with wisdom that is eternal

Help me in the circle made.

I appeal to the Lord and lady to consider my request

I am calling to me the element water.

The ancients are my inspiration that bear the truth from beyond

Make sure you're present tonight and be sure to stay long.

Lady and Lord I pray that you keep me safe and near by your side

The elemental quality of water make me feel full of feelings of pride.

Let the old ones be patient with me and give me patience that will last

Be present throughout the night as you join the circle that we will.

I call the lord and lady who gave me my birth,

I appeal to the earth element

For me to be awash with their beautiful shining.

Lord and Lady, protect and shield me from harm with your love.

Therefore, the earth inspires me both above and below.

I pray that the wise old men give me wisdom that will last,

Help me with this circle make.

I am calling you with complete desire

Call me to the element of fire.

I ask the wise ones to be forever wise and ancient

To soothe me to me, quiet longings and listen to my crying.

Please protect me, Lord and lady, by using your ability to heal

Fire may be my protection beyond the steel's strength

I hope that the older ones will grant me the wisdom to last

Also, grant me access to the circle that I cast."

Feel free to try this ritual or design one on your own with this template as a basis.

Concept of Evocation Concept of Evocation

Evocation is a practice of spirituality that allows you to make a call to or summon spirits (benign or malignant) to appear outside of your body, in the form of energy. It's a method used to connect with your ancestral relatives or friends for the first time. The rituals invoke awe to learn about the true nature of spirits and to get familiar with the spirit before allowing them into your life. The spirits and familiars get closer to us over time but only when a connection is established.

When you invoke, there is no direct connection with the entity being summoned. It is not in direct the physical appearance even though you can sense and feel its presence. They cannot control the us or manipulate us or control our vitality as they do not have our explicit consent. Certain magical traditions conduct ceremonies of evocation that make use of mind-altering substances , either with or without utterances.

Manuals such as Lemegeton, Claviculis Salomonis, and the Sacred Magic of Abra Melin the Mage give specific instructions and devotions to summoning one or more entities, deceased relatives and other spirits that are familiar to you.

The manuals described in these documents, the entities were controlled using long Hellenic and Kabbalistic rituals in the names of God. The summoner also employed weapons, staves, wands incense, intricate diagrams written on parchment or on other surfaces and daggers.

Enochian magic can be invoked using crystal balls or mirrors. The seer or volunteer is in tune with the voice of the entity and may relay necessary messages to the person who invokes. Sometimes, the volunteer acts as a mediumwho speaks on behalf of the entity, not for it. In certain instances the entity could be contained in a symbol artifact or transformed into a form or diagram that it is unable to be escaped without their explicit authorization.

In occult practice Evocations can be used to summon a demon, sublunary, or other unpredictably entity. The Salomonis Regis, or Lesser Key of King Solomon There are specific instructions for practitioners to summon demonic evocations. The method is an ethereal triangle that is drawn to contain the entity being evoked and an enchanted circle that is sealed for the protection of the summoner.

The issue with this is that the repeated repetition of the ritual for long time periods can put you at risk of becoming the character of the character that you subconsciously invoke. Similar to how we mimic the actions of the people whom we have the most affinity with. If this occurs with the context of spirituality it is the person summoning or occultist's duty to stay conscious of these subconscious influences. They are the ones who have to draw the line which they should not overstep unless they intend to take in the qualities of this spirit forever. This is the reason why occultists should have greater control over their mind than people of average age.

The difference between Evocation and Invocation

Invoking the entity's name is to summon it into your life. This lets you assume any or all of its traits or the essence. You are a part of the person or entity you are calling upon. It is a very intimate process, and the outcomes are a greater level of power and communication.

Invocations require the summoner transform into the medium. The person summoned is supposed to arise from within the person who summoned them. Invoking, must use all your resources and energy to make sure it happens. When you have succeeded in your prayer the spirit will act through the person who summons. Many changes could occur in the form of vocal change to physical appearance and manner of speaking. A lot of people who have been in these posts are said they are aware of the entity that is using them as a vehicle. Other suffer extreme dissociation and gaps in time.

Evocation is different in that the summoner conjures an entity to obtain a specific benefit or information, or a purpose that is aimed at achieving in the physical realm. Once the task is completed the person summoned may decide to bind, banish, or dispel the entity. There isn't any obligation or supplication for the entity. The intention is to have the entity provide favors or answers to questions. The person summoned may choose to offer an offering to the entity in a gesture of it is a courtesy requirement. Essential to summoning is the distance that is created by the practitioner between the summoner and the entity.

To invoke, Evoke or both?

There are many ways of activating and activating spirits. The most commonly used include visualisation, Ouija boards, automatic writing, pendulums and dreams. The decision of whether to invoke or evoke depends on the subject and the character of the entity. With humans too there are various degrees of interactions, all based on your level of intimacy to the person. It's not like you would hug a stranger who isn't in the street do you?

If you were to invoke or invoke any entity, for instance Mammon for instance Would you like to summon him since you're in love with money but have not learned the full implications of working with Mammon? Don't forget that a single-minded obsession can be unhealthy and affect your judgment and blind you to the cost for certain choices. What happens if, once you've become wealthy and filthy, you find that it is no longer able to hold the attraction and importance it once did? What happens next? You're enslaved to the demon that you summoned.

When you are dipping your toes into summoning or embodying an individual spirit, you should consider every option. It's not a good idea to invoke entities solely because you have the information or think that it's a great idea for your summer vacation because this "cool" idea could quickly become a mess. These are issues that require serious consideration. Before you attempt to invoke or invoke, make sure that the characteristics of the entity align with your requirements. Your ultimate goals should be considered first. Do not put your horse before your cart. The Wiccan Rede could allow you to do as you want, but be ready for the consequences.

Beyond your goals It is important to think about your skills. It's been said, "Where attention goes, energy flows." Engaging with supernatural forces and energies can be exciting enjoyable, rewarding, and impressive, but caution must be taken into consideration. An understanding of the various rituals and powers is essential as is a positive attitude. If you don't have these two, it can put you in a position that you're confronted with a lot of energy that you don't have the least idea of about how to deal with.

Budding occultists are wondering if they could invoke and call forth simultaneously. It's possible. But does it really matter? In this case, for instance, you would like to invoke and invoke Orobas or the Goetic entity. Invoking Orobas is to embody his wisdom and power to win over the hearts of enemies and friends alike. He will remain committed to you, to reveal answers to your questions about the past, present and the future, and shield yourself from harm and attraction of other forces. In truth, you're creating an uncontrollable storm in the teacup.

Invocation already has the effects of evocation, to a certain extent. The effect on the physical plane can be seen in both instances. The distinction is that evocation blocks you from being the persona you've invoked. Then, what happens if decide to invoke a spirit but call forth another.

Let's call Orobas for a second time and then invoke another entity, like Astaroth. Both are powerful and their strengths are negligible one another. The former requires you to demonstrate honesty while the latter thought through his own personal beliefs which might or not align to the reality.

The only rule that says it's permissible for two people to be summoned at time is that their abilities match each other to achieve your objectives. Therefore instead of

Astaroth You invoke Andromalius. His exemplary ways of punishing criminals and dealers who are dishonest add to Orobas's integrity.

Whatever you do, do not attempt to summon more than one entity at the beginning of your journey. There's a lot instruction required to successfully call, control, tie an entity, or even exile it. Further training and experience is required to convince entities to yield more power or offering greater favors than they normally will. Inexperience or distractions during invocations/evocations will make you powerful spiritual enemies, leaving you bound in a pact that you never bargained for or imagined. In this regard, do not refocus your energy and energy between multiple things and entities at once.

Chapter 9: Crystal Magic And Alchemy

For centuries crystals, regardless of their dimensions, have been considered as a gift from the Gods to the human race. As humans, they possess unique energy vibrations. They can be used as a whole or to enhance your magical abilities. Many crystals are available, many have overlapping functions and properties. You can buy them on the internet and through New Age shops, or at fairs of spirit. They can also be given as a giftor find them in a riverbed, quarry or on a walk in the woods. In this section we'll look at various stones that are versatile and their healing properties and their metaphysical significance.

Crystal Energy is a variety of forms. Crystal Energy

Projective Crystals: They are similar to Yang energy. They radiate energy and are masculine and are linked to fire and air elements as evidenced by their vivid colours, sounds, and energy. They usually have colors that are associated with sunlight or blood with gold, red as well as orange and yellow shades. They are excellent for healing and protecting against negative energy. They are essential stones to possess when you are you need an increase in willpower energy, vitality, self-confidence power, and determination. Examples include tiger's eye, bloodstone, ruby, carnelian, citrine, red jasper, amber, cinnabar, onyx, et cetera.

Receptive Crystals: They are linked to Yin energy. The crystals are absorbing energy, and feminine and closely related with the elemental elements like earth and water. These stones provide the feeling of calm spiritual grounding and the enhancement in psychic powers. They are a shade of the cooler end of the spectrum of colors, including silver, purple, blue white, green, grey, brown and pink. They are excellent for enhancing the sense of peace, love, compassion psychic powers, and improving the state of mind. In this section, the most sought-after crystals are moonstone, turquoise malachite, lapis-lazuli, malachite Jade, Rose Quartz Labradorite, aqua Aura Chrysocolla, and so on.

Certain crystals are not in the category. They possess dual properties of reception and projection based on the type of crystal and the energy you connect to during spell work. Clear quartz gold healer quartz amethyst, opal, ametrine and numerous black crystals belong to this category of dual-power, too. As you learn and do more crystal work you are more aware of the power crystals carry.

The most versatile stones you can own.

Amethyst: A variation from the Quartz family of stones, its colors vary from lilac through a royal purple. The main feature of this stone is its color zoning. As parts of the gem are characterized by an angular zone that range from light to darker colors similar to the appearance of ombre. The name derives by the Greek amethystos, which means "not drunk." This is due to the fact that the belief was that this gem was placed in an end of the drink glass was able to keep its owner away from being drunk.

Alchemical Properties Amethyst water balances hormones, cleanses blood, eases stress and pain. Additionally, it stimulates the nervous system and helps to maintain sobriety. A night of sleep with amethyst on your pillow can help you sleep better and assists you in understanding your desires.

Mystical Properties Stones are connected to the angel Raphael. It can absorb negativity. Its electromagnetic frequencies assist in meditation as well as manifestation and spiritual awakening. Its connection to the chakra of the crown, the soma the third eye, the stellar gateway helps to awaken your intuition and psychic powers. It also removes illusions that block you from being able to see the truth.

Black Tourmaline or Schorl: A piezoelectric and pyroelectric rock composed of sodium iron borate silicate. It is famous for its role in drawing the ash of pipes from ancient times.

The Alchemical properties: it helps strengthen the thyroid gland, immune system as well as neural networks. It helps improve hand-eye coordination, improves spinal alignment, eases discomfort, eases inflammation and protects against motion sickness. Tourmaline minimizes the negative effect of electromagnetic and geomagnetic energy. It can also improve circulation, immunity and metabolism, as well as help reduce pain in the lungs, lung issues and muscle aches.

Mystical Properties: As a grounding stone, it can dispel negative behavior patterns and evil entities. It also provides psychic protection and can be used in scrying, protection and purification rituals.

Bloodstone: Also known as heliotrope with hues ranging between dark green and deep blue and dots of rust or red, it was believed to arise from the droplets of blood that dropped from Jesus on jasper stones near the at the foot of the cross.

Alchemical Properties: A powdered bloodstones when mixed with egg whites and honey could remove snake venom, and stop the growth of tumors and bleeding. (That is why you should visit your physician in the event that you suffer from one of these symptoms and take the bloodstone as an alternative treatment.) It improves physical stamina it cleanses kidneys and blood, and decreases the frequency of nosebleeds, acidity and pus release.

The Mystical Property: This aids in psychic healing, boosts Kundalini, enhances manifestation, is compatible with weather magic and wards off negative energy.

Carnelian (also known as Singer's Stone: Ancient Egyptians called this crystal "the the setting sun" because of its deep amber or reddish orange color.

The Alchemical properties: it aids in the absorption of minerals and vitamins and also strengthens bones and ligaments. It eases arthritis, depression, rheumatism lower back issues boosts libido and increases fertility. If it's pulverized, carnelian can heal gum and tooth inflammations. Consult your dentist in case you're suffering from these.

The Mystical properties of it can restore the spirit, motivation and creativity. It also provides relief from abuse of all kinds It boosts self-esteem and lessens jealousy. It is often used in amulets and talismans to stop psychic attacks and rekindle the passion that has been lost.

Citrine The Citrine is a rare stone that belongs in the quartz family. Its hue is a mix of golden yellow and reddish-orange or orange-brown.

Alchemical Properties: It's an immune booster and hormone balancer. It helps fight degenerative illnesses chronic fatigue, degenerative diseases, and urinary tract infections. The spleen is aided by citrine-infused water as well as the pancreas. It also helps relieve menstrual cramps.

Mystical properties: This cleanses of negative thoughts that attract abundance and wealth as well as boosts self-esteem and self-confidence. It assists in overcoming fears and anxiety, decreases the anxiety and fear of criticism to transform negative energies into positive.

Clear Quartz Clear Quartz is the reason for the term "crystal," from the Greek word "krystallos," meaning, "clear clear ice." The ancient Greeks believed that the Gods who froze celestial water created quartz. It is believed to be proof that cities like Atlantis and Lemuria were in existence.

Alchemical Properties The alchemical properties cleanse organs and encourages cell regeneration and oxygenation of tissues. It helps improve bone, joints and connective tissue. helps heal blockages, blisters, and strengthens the body's vibrational structure.

Mystical Properties The Mystical Properties stone is easily programmed and flexible stone. It increases the vibrational energy of your body and psychic energy and increases your awareness and removes negative energy. It increases the determination, focus and power of the other crystals. It assists with the recall of past lives, and allows the communication of animals, spirits guides familiars, as well as plants. Clear quartz also improves the endurance of people, their patience and prosperity.

Hematite is a mineral that's formed by the oxidation of iron and is available in a wide range of colors that range from brown to red gray, and black. The name comes of its Greek phrase "haimatites," an allusion to its rusty red color. According to Greek legend the origin of the name was after Saturn killed Uranus, his dad. Uranus.

Alchemical Properties It's an effective blood cleanser that helps the nervous system and heart and boosts circulation. It eliminates cravings that stem from unfulfilled desires and emotional cravings. It helps to reduce inflammation.

Mystical properties: It helps improve concentration and focus, boosts confidence in yourself and your charisma, and protects from mental, physical and psychological problems, and is an excellent stone to ground.

Jade is highly regarded among Chinese as well as Aztecs as a luck charm, Jade is a transparent or translucent stone that has colors that range between dark-green to grey yellow, brown even black.

The Alchemical properties: it relieves physical pain, speeds up healing following surgery, increases skin elasticity, helps prevent wrinkles, removes blood toxins, and helps to promote the growth of plants as well as harmony, love and prosperity. Its muscle relaxant properties aid with respiratory problems.

Mystical properties: it assists recall dreams, removes negativity it helps to gain clarity and clarity in relationships that are toxic, enhances confidence in self-confidence and meditation, and helps to cleanse energy fields.

Jet: It is neither a crystal nor mineral, it's a mineraloid derived by fossilized driftwood. It went through extreme pressure and then decayed to result in a dark brown solid that has metallic luster that is like coal.

Chemical Properties of Alchemical: This eases the symptoms of altitude sickness infection, bacterial and viral and speeds up DNA repair and helps with migraines or headaches as well as dental pain and stomach pain.

Mystical properties: it offers psychic security, stabilizes and shields businesses from losses, dispels envy, aids in grounding, increases psychic power, increases the kundalini chakra, guards against pain, violence sleepless nights, vampire energy and even bottled emotions.

Lapis Lazuli is a symbol of cosmic connection Lazurite is also known as a symbol of cosmic correspondence. the stone is available in a variety of shades of blue that range from light to indigo. It's a blend from three different minerals: pyrite lazurite and calcite. It is valued higher than gold itself, Lapis is one of the oldest sought-after stones on Earth.

Alchemical Properties can strengthen the immune system. It regulates menstrual cycles and relieves pain, lowers blood pressure as well as cleanses the body. It provides relief from insomnia, attention deficit disorders and vertigo, as well as helps treat disorders of the larynx, throat and the vocal cord.

Mystical properties: It helps to promote the ease of communication, inner observation authenticity, truth, psychic protection the ability to see clearly, with compassion and wisdom. It is used in talismans to encourage friendship and loyalty and to enhance psychic ability.

Malachite The sparkling green, or brightly green crystal that has been formed by the carbonate of copper.

The Alchemical properties: it eliminates electromagnetic and radiation pollution assists the liver to detoxify and helps treat female reproductive issues such as menstrual cramps. It is used to treat vertigo, dyslexia and aerophobia. It also treats carsickness epilepsy, arthritis and pancreas diseases and the spleen. It treats joint fractures, joint pains and tumors.

Mystical Properties: Sometimes referred to as the stone of transformation It improves insight and dispels psychic imbalance. It absorbs negative energy and is utilized for prosperity spells. It also encourages compassion, reduces the fear of confrontation, and dissolves emotional trauma, toxic patterns blocks, residues, and blockages from previous lives. It is toxic when it is used in large amounts.

Moonstone or Traveler's stone: Opalescent, translucent crystal blue variation of the mineral orthoclase feldspar It is naturally found in areas in India in India and Sri Lanka.

Alchemical Properties The Alchemical Properties regulate your female reproductive system. It strengthens pituitary glands, hormonesand stomach and digestive systems, it also decreases weight gain and edema.

Spiritual Properties: This boosts psychic abilities and intuition. It aids in tapping to your feminine energy, helps to combat stress, ego anger, materialism and stress as well as supplying you with energetic cosmic energy. To achieve this, consider investing in stones that are grounded such as Hematite in order to absorb the moonstone's energies.

Obsidian is a silica-rich igneous rock made of volcanic lava. It is black in color and with a sparkling shimmer, shamans see it as a portal across the space and time. It's also known as royal agate, glass-agate as well as volcanic glass. Blue, snowflake, apache tear and mahogany obsidians are more gentle than black versions.

Chemical Properties of Alchemical: Utilized for making tools for cutting and piercing such as surgical scalpels. It also heals injuries to the ear, fractures as well as sciatica, spinal disorders and Alopecia. It improves the lymphatic and immune systems.

The Mystical Property: This aids in deep soul healing, by uncovering character flaws, clearing the negative structures, boosts self-assurance confidence, self-control, strength and awareness, as well as psychic protection. It also absorbs negative energies from the outside and helps to activate energy sources that are not being utilized. It is employed to scrying, grounding, meditation, and centering as well as in the making of athames.

Rose Quartz is known as the stone of love unconditionally it is a pale blush or rose-colored hue. It is because of deposits of manganese, iron or titanium.

The Alchemical properties: it soothes breathing issues, increases circulation, reduces tension and heart palpitations. It eases anxiety disorders and Alzheimer's disease, fatigue, and dementia. It also treats burns, bruisesand kidney disease, infertility as well as migraines. It also shields against environmental pollutants.

The Mystical Property: It eases trust problems in relationships, and soothes emotional pain, grief as well as trauma from past and current lives. It unlocks the heart chakra on all levels to allow and receive affection. It promotes happiness, peace, self-worth, comfort and healing.

"Tiger's eye" or Wolf Stone: A metamorphic rock belonging to the chalcedony family that has a smooth luster it comes in a variety of colors, ranging from brown to red to gold.

The Alchemical properties: it decreases the depression and blood pressure, increases night vision, aids digestion, helps strengthen and align the spine, flushes out toxic substances, heals fractures, regulates mood swings, boosts the bloodstream, improves fertility and relieves constriction in the gallbladder and stomach.

Mystical properties: It calms the mind, improves mental clarity, and decreases appetite cravings, eating disorders and cravings. It enhances dream recall meditation capabilities and also stimulates the kundalini. It also balances Yin and Yang energies and the brain hemispheres.

There is no need to buy all of these items all at one time. Begin with the ones that are appealing to you and then add them the collection. Charge and clean your crystals prior to and after you purchase them or use them. When charging crystals, certain experts recommend charging stones using fire energy , such as bloodstones, citrine, carnelians and obsidian by using sunlight. Stones that have water energy such as lapis-lazuli, jade moonstone as well as jet, are charged by moonlight. Stones that are based on earth like jasper, hematite malachite, green jade tourmaline, and tiger eyes are charged by placing them in earth.

Be aware that these are just ideas. A thorough investigation must be conducted in regards to cleaning, charging and using crystals for magical or medicinal uses. Amazonite and cinnabar, malachite and emerald and azurite, for instance, are poisonous when inhaled. Hematite, selenite and Kunzite and ulexite disintegrate in water. The turquoise and pearl disappear with exposure to water. Citrine, amethystand rose quartz, and aventurine may fade after long-term exposure to sunlight. Beware of carrying wireless devices like smartphones around charged stones since they can disrupt their magic field.

A few Spells to Crystal Magic

House Blessings or Consecrating the Space that is sacred Space

You'll require:

* A single white candle.

A single or multiple amethyst or quartz crystals.

* Myrrh or lemon essential oils (place one drop of the oil in each crystal).

Place the stones next to the candle lit, and imagine the white light emanating out of it, covering every inch of your home or area. Make affirmations such as "I declare this house or space to be a sacred space. Joy well-being, prosperity, and happiness are plentiful in this space. Thus, let that it is." After that you can allow the candle to die completely on its own. Set the amethyst in an area that is prominent in your home or in your living space to continue radiating positive energy.

Financial Aid Crystal Spell

You'll require:

1. A wealth crystal that you like (jade carnelian, citrine, pyrite, moss , or jade).

Notepads or a piece of paper with an ink pen.

A green candle.

Make a candle light and write your name and the specific requirement on the notepad or paper, and the amount you need to meet the requirement. For instance, "$5,000 monthly." Do not use words such as

"I want" or "I want" as this spell can increase the energy of that spell, ensuring you will always have what you need or.

The paper is folded into a square and place the crystal on top and say, "I thank the universe for the blessings it provides, and through the help of this (name that the crystal bears) I invoke the answer to my problems." Keep the stone placed on paper till the candle is burned out, then put it into the ground in a potted plant or within your property. Be sure to remember where this place is. Make a note of it should you need to. Place the stone in the ground until you have achieved your goal and then remove the paper and crystal. Thank the universe for fulfilling your dream. Being grateful will give you the strength to perform the future.

Chapter 10: Designing Your Rituals And

Spells

Expert spell makers have a solid understanding of the magic principles and comprehend the energy flow in the universe. Spellcrafting can teach you how to best use the power of nature, knowing when the best moment to cast your spell, how you can increase your level of energy, and the nuances and ethics of fine-tuning existing spells. As you become more adept you will discover that personally designed spells do more than aid in the development of your craft, but also help you improve your practice.

Crafting Your Spells

There are two options for making spells. One is to choose an existing one and modify it according to your own requirements. It is possible to modify certain elements provided that the substitutes don't deviate from the intention that the magic spell is aiming for. The gods can be changed or specific words rewritten in accordance with your tradition or religious convictions. The idea is to draw as much energy as you can but still keeping the original form of the spell.

The other option is to create own spell completely from scratch. If you can't locate a spell that is suitable for your requirements or when existing ones appear to be missing something. Before making this move, some research to discover the right connections and ingredients to integrate in your work. Examples of correspondences include : herbs oil, gods incense, offering and planets, as well as elements and colors. The more precise and accurate your letters are stronger your magic will be.

Whatever your chosen method, whether it's either a new or previously created spell the next step to complete is to create an incantation to express your intention. Incantations can be poetic or not have any rhyme whatsoever. Incantations generally include prayers to gods whose power coincide with your goals. Incantation with rhyme is traditional and considered to be more powerful because of the inherent magic in rhyme. In the words of Gwen Thompson said in the 1975 issue of Green

Egg, "To bind the spell, every time it is best to allow the spell to be spoken using rhyme."

Methods to create a foolproof Spell

Step 1. Be Clear about Your Wish It is not worth casting a spell just to get it done. It's an unnecessary waste of time. When you are creating spells, it is important to be able to think about what you'd like to accomplish. Successful spells require precise goals. If you don't have this in mind, you're shooting your towards a vague goal that results in only limited success. To become a master craftsman You must define your objectives by sorting through superficial thoughts and then determining what you'd like.

Make sure your goals are achievable and your spells should be precise. It's not necessary to rhyme. Some people aren't able to grasp the art to write verse. Let's take a look at how beginning or intermediate spell-crafters can write financial aid spells.

Beginner: I'll need some more cash in matter of minutes.

Intermediate: Provide me with the opportunity to work in a job that is regular and secure raises of not less than $X per year with frequent promotions.

Master: Create opportunities to secure and stable income streams, with a pay that is not less than $X per month after all bills, expenses or investments are taken care of.

The newbie demanded more money within a short time. This can open the door to practically anything that can provide a bit more than it did before. They might find a $20 bill in their pockets or receive a one-dollar gift card. This isn't what they had hoped for however, it's not a bad thing also, as per the sleight of hand.

For the intermediate caster, it is possible to have a steady job. It is possible to get a occasional raise but the chance of costs eating away at the increase in income is. Each time a salary or raise arrives and boom! The expenses pour down like hailstones, and there's no savings left to.

The master spell allows you to draw in all streams of income, ensuring the flow of money is steady rather than an unintentional magic trick. The spell was created to prevent the possibility of emergencies that could consume the money you've earned.

Step 2. Consider the energies You'd like to harness and the desired result before writing your spell Consider the possibility of coordinating your timing to coincide with lunar phases, astrological influences and planetary times to enhance the effectiveness of your spell.

The ancient Sumerians along with Orthodox magicians developed rituals and ceremonies centered around these five elements (water air, earth and fire). They believed that each element had powerful symbolic meaning. Ether is also referred to as spirit because it is believed to be the non-material representation of gods angels, spirits, angels and other celestial entities.

Step 3. Enhance the power of the spell by being in a calm state of mind: agitated states aren't effective in releasing energy and harnessing it. To write a spell, you need to shift your mind to make it quiet the back of your head.

Step 4. Lift and release energy towards Your Goal The real base of casting spells. Spells gain power through the energy you use as well as the ingredients you choose for the spell.

Step 5. Make Your Goal Manifest This is the most important step the last stage of casting spells.

Spells can be used to resolve a variety of issues. But, there are many books that focus on spells that address the everyday demands, such as security and security, love, wealth and healing. One reason for failure in prosperity and abundance spells is that they are driven by emotions of envy, lust, or greed. It is clear casting spells to resolve financial issues is understandable. However there are certain requirements that are justified but some aren't. This isn't because they aren't there however, the reason for this is that their absence is rooted in emotions and emotions that are more powerful than you realize.

You are able to cast spells at any time that is your pleasure so long as you're:

* In the right mindset Distractions and worries alter the mind's focus which weakens the effects that the magic spell has. Repressing emotional reactions, such as

anger, guilt or fear. This puts the possibility of granting orders on the instantaneous that are not only reckless, but also comes with unanticipated and unexpected consequences.

"In Excellent Health" A poor health is an indication of energy imbalance. Magick is a tough job. Therefore, it would be helpful to have the ability to tap into the power of. The ability to harness power is a requirement to remain at the highest level of health. It is impossible for anyone to perform any activity to the very best of their ability when they are seriously ill. It's a false assumption to believe we can bring about positive changes when we are unwell. The only exemption to casting spells for ill health is when they are aimed to boost your energy levels. In this case, you should use more calm spells, which require a more gentle method of harnessing the power of magic.

When you are formulating spells, be aware that all the details are crucial including the color of the candle and shape, the circular pattern on the ground and the pronunciation of the names, the herbs the day or hour that you are facing when chanting, as well as any essential oils or incense used are crucial. Try to make sure you have it right or make use of the correct equivalents for every spell.

The significance of correspondence in Spell Crafting

When creating spells it is essential to have correspondence. The correspondences used in Wicca are items, symbols or times that are aligned with certain magical vibrations or energies. Correspondence doesn't work as magic; rather, it enhances magic, so that spells can be strengthened by visualisation and intention.

Use of letters is an art that has been around since the beginning of time. It is believed that the more of it is integrated into spells, the higher chances that it will be effective. For instance, if casting a spell to boost creativity using candles in orange are the ideal. Alongside oils such as cedarwood oil as well as crystals like Herkimer diamond or pyrite, you could benefit from chanting the gods of creativity such as Athena, Hephaestus, or Kvasir. Spells to boost creativity should be performed in the phase of the moon that is waxing or full to boost the odds of success.

Writing your spells will allow you to consider and think about. It is only through research that to are aware of what each item, phrase, and element represents. Knowing the significance behind each word spoken and each action executed will help you focus your intention which is the primary magical element of the ability to cast spells.

How to Ensure Ethics of Spellcasting

Spellcasters are often criticized. Spellcasters are accused of utilizing power for personal profit. This isn't an attribute associated with only pagans or witches. People tend to throw ethics to the wind if they are in the market for something. Real magicians realize that magic comes with consequences. Morality prevents them from achieving dominance in the world as we understand it. The fact that they work in secret doesn't necessarily mean that they don't adhere to a moral code that they follow.

If you've made it to this point, you already know that just because you're able to summon gods doesn't mean that you're allowed to take over Cartier's store or rob banks. These aren't ethical goals which undermine the fundamentals of the practice of casting spells. Imagine if all of the world chose to utilize the power of their own.

When you craft spells it is essential to know the morally acceptable and what is not. Your views should be in line or else ethics will become untrue. If you're against casting spells of love one day and you are to the bottom of an elixir of love the next day, this can lead to inconsistent views. The skepticism can be seen when you lash out at someone else who has the same actions as you do.

The concept of provisional ethics is often a necessity since you might be in a position to select between two choices, so pick the less harmful option. Sometimes, the advantages of many overshadow the desires of a select very few. In the end, your moral code will force you to consider your actions to promote magic, and to take responsibility for them.

Be aware of the importance of freewill when it comes to magic. When writing spells, don't cast any spell that deprives someone else of their freedom. A rule of thumb to follow when crafting spells is that spells should work in harmony with the natural sequence of events not against them. This is the only way to ensure they are as effective as you would like to see them be and the chance of making mistakes in judgement is reduced.

Ethics-related Outs

A lot of spell books recommend including a postscript to spells that are cast to protect you from any consequences. The most commonly used one is "by the freewill of everyone to do no harm." This sentence is a powerful way to reinforce your innocence of intention and guards against the clauses that spells that you intentionally do not want to be. Keep this in mind and be aware that the intention motivation, motive, and reasoning behind a spell can be considered more than just a codicil at its conclusion, which relieves you from accountability.

Websites and books on occultism are unable to provide many clues. You must learn to be confident in yourself and your abilities. Just because a sentence is recorded in numerous texts doesn't mean it is perfect. If something doesn't feel right for you during your spellwork, don't feel scared to alter it. Though, in many cases correspondences such as the lunar, time, and gods are considered because of their relationship to the intent of the spell, altering one aspect without full knowledge of the motive behind the spell may result in the spell losing its power.

In the spell-crafting process is the notion of responsibility which is the natural partner to power. It is not possible to control the power and transfer the responsibility to someone else. Every action is accompanied by consequences therefore, if you choose to cast spells, you must be ready to face the consequences (if there is any) from the spell. Before writing, you should take the time to gather the most information you can regarding the scenario.

Be sure to think twice before you apply the pen to paper will ensure that you don't create unintentional or impulsive phrases. Even in situations that are time-sensitive it is important to remain at peace and calm.

Make rough notes, then re-read your notes repeatedly to determine if you find yourself in the same position regarding the situation, or if you've gained an entirely new perspective. If you make the decision to hurt another person in a fit of fury, be sure that you're prepared to endure it if someone else harms you back. The web of energy that connects us all is never boring.

Seal your spell. This is an essential part of rituals, which reinforces the purpose of your spell. A lot of Wiccan spell books advise you to use the phrase "so moot it is" which is an overly formal method of saying "may that be" as in "somote" or "amen" to Christians as well as the "selah" in the case of Jews. Make your seal by stating something as basic as "it has been completed." This will send an indication to your subconscious and conscious subconscious mind to say that this spell has been completed and all you need to do is believe in the universe to change the energy to your benefit.

Timing can be a bit tricky but it is helpful in optimizing your spells. If you're in immediate requirement, create a fast spell. It's not written in stone that specific spells should be done at a certain time, or even not at all. If your spell works best at night when the moon's at its fullest and you are in urgent requirement, why wait until an eclipsing moon? Sure, certain times of the moon can increase or enhance the effectiveness of spells However, if you're in the middle of a dark night and you're required the power of a spell in order to help a pet who appears to be at its last, then by all means, go ahead. Healing can happen anytime, day or time or lunar phase.

There is no magic that will make you eternally young or unnoticeable. They are unattainable targets. When creating a spell, the best practice is to ensure that it is possible without the help of magic. Perform magic in order to make accomplishing these goals more simple.

To become a skilled spell maker, you have to make sure you keep accurate notes. Making spells is similar to cooking or chemistry. It is best if you would keep tweaking your skills to achieve the best results. The only way to see how far your talent has improved is by note-taking and record-keeping. Notes of what you used and in what proportions the time it took for the spell to take effect and so on can aid you when you'll need to duplicate it for your own benefit or for to benefit someone else.

The records also let you examine new strategies you've discovered or developed, instances when your powers are at their highest; the things you have to modify to alter the result of any spell and how to best rewrite errors in your spells.

Your records should contain the following information:

* The date and time the spell was cast.
* The direction in which it was done.
* The current weather conditions.
* The entire text of the spell.
* Ingredients that are required.
* Your feelings at the moment.
* Results for both short and long-term.
* Any other information that is pertinent.

If you have added something new during the course of a spell, make note of the change. Note down astrological details during the day during the spell. Also, note especially if there was anything you didn't include or you discovered a method to improve the effectiveness of a spell. Notes like these are valuable to refer to in the future when you develop as a caster or crafter.

Chapter 11: Tools Of The Craft

The tools and practices differ in accordance with tradition and even from witches to witches. The fact is, tools can help to harness magic energy However, they are not mandatory. The most essential tool for spellwork is the caster's will without which all other things are inactive. Here are some tools that you can begin with. It is not necessary to have every one of these. You can use your imagination when casting. Do not allow the lack of a device to hinder you from doing magic.

Beginner Magic Tools

Athame or Athalme Pronounced A-Tham-ay, it is a sacred blade that symbolizes masculinity and fire, which is the element that represents it and, in certain covens it's air as the air element. It is known as Yag-dirk by Saxons the blade is black with a black hilt. It is a double-edged blade that is often shaped in a crescent to symbolize the moon. It can be employed to guide magical energy, create ritual circles, ward off negative energies, and perform invocations. The athame is not considered a cutting instrument however it can be made to be engraved with sigils or runes. Certain witches of the family believe that athames should not be made from metal because it interferes the earth's energy. To avoid this, traditional witches craft athames out of flant.

Bells: They are often found in Pagan practices. The bell's shape is reminiscent of the old images of the human genitalia. the handle is a representation of the phallus, and the body represents a the vulva. Some symbologists believe that the bell's body is symbolic of the womb, and the handle is the child that lives within. In this way, the majority of Wiccan bells are designed to mimic the shape of the female.

Witches make use of smaller bells with handles to ward off from the eye of evil, calling or banishing entities and conducting cleansing rituals, aiding healing, and strengthening fertility spells. Bells that are placed on the floor or in entrances are used as protection amulets or guard dogs to warn against the evil spirits. Certain sects drink potions from the bell's cup because they believe it can enhance the potency of herbal teas.

Bolline is a knife utilized to cut through spells and other magical rituals. It is typically white-handled and double-edged, as opposed to the athame. The bolline is an everyday knife, or an athame as a ritual knife. The various colors of the handles permit easy identification and also prevent the desecration of the athame. It is possible to use a standard knife to make the Bolline. Bollines are employed for chopping herbs, carving inscribed inscriptions and cutting fabrics thread, cords, or thread.

A Broomstick, also known as a Besom is the main altar tools used in witchcraft. It is a symbol of the male and female energies. The stick represents the male energy that is inserted into straw or female twigs. Witchcraft has been associated with Brooms since ancient times, with the belief that they were used as transport tools. Brooms function as a way for transferring between realms and one that follows and clean the area of energetic and physical waste.

They can also be used to clean up footprints since footprints left behind can be vulnerable to the effects of evil magic. Anyone who wants to cause harm can use the footprints left behind. Brooms are among the most sacred characteristics of Hecate and, in the present they are the symbol of witchcraft and are proudly used by Wiccans to honor the times of fire. They are easy to make however there are some stunning ones that are available on online shops for crafts like Etsy. Traditional besoms have an the handle of ash as well as willow bindings. an birch brush. However, it is best to use tools that are that are available, just like the rest of your tools.

of Shadows: Book of Shadows: A book filled with magical texts and directions utilized in various Pagan religious practices, and Wicca also, to note down rituals, spells and other invocations.

Burine It is not to be confused with diuretic pills It is a tool that is sharp and employed by witches to create symbols, words or designs into supernatural objects. Burines could be nails pins as well as crystal point.

Candles and Incense Candles and Incense: They are essential to witchcraft, and are the subject of a whole area dedicated to their research. They are both inexpensive and easy to find, and ideal for witches living at home to do their work in a relaxed manner.

Compass: A lot of rituals and energy alignment practices use using the 4 cardinal directions and a witch who isn't spatially conscious needs the aid of a compass to ensure that she is orientated correctly.

Crystals: They serve as tools for psychic use and also as psychic materials. Crystals of different types are associated with various powers and elements. They are employed in many rituals, from forming sacred circles, cleaning and charging other magical tools, and to help you remain in the flow during spellwork.

Cards: They are widely used as tool for casting spells and divination. There are various cards to use to help with meditation, divination and various other purposes, but Tarot cards are the most well-known divination cards. In the Middle Ages, Christians called them the Devil's Picture Book and considered their presence in homes as a sign of sin. They were invented within East Asia, there is there is still some debate about the authenticity of these cards. Chinese as well as Korean in their origins. Tarot suits are akin to many magical devices such as the pentacle, chalice and other such. The oldest surviving tarot deck that is available today is called the Visconti-Sforza.

Cauldrons: The phrase "cauldron" is derived of the Latin "caldarium," meaning "hot bath." It represents the water element as well as female energy. It also symbolizes the universal womb as well as resurrection. In the ancient Egyptian hieroglyphics the symbol of females was a vessel. The most well-known cauldron of all time is the Gunderstrup gilded in silver Cauldron from 1891. It is stored in the National Museum of Copenhagen.

Cauldrons are utilized in spells to make potions that contain flames, candles that burn cooking food, creating medicines, and performing destructive magic. For example the act of covering a poppet with one can be interpreted as a way of burying the enemy. Cast iron is traditionally the preferred metal however other metals like porcelain, ceramic as well as brass and copper are also possible. Make sure your pot is protected from corrosion by coating it with oil or grease and then heating it to temperatures of 375°F for one hour. If your cauldron is in a state of rust it is possible to use the Coca-Cola technique. Add some to the cauldron overnight and allow it to sit. Clean it with steel wool on the following day.

Goblet or Chalice: A cup of water or vessel that is a representation of the element of water, this is a symbol for femininity or of the Goddess's womb. It typically, it is made of silver in order to represent the lunar energy. The most well-known chalice of all has to be one that is known as the Holy Grail. Sharing a chalice at a time of ceremonies with coveners shows the unity and a sense of purpose. Chalices can also be made from the indigo-colored glass, or even crystal. It is believed that the Great Wiccan Rite is celebrated by immersing an athame in an Chalice.

Cords: The knots and cords are used for many purposes. Small cords are utilized in knot spells that bring forth an intention, command, or wish. Knots can also be used for protection, sex, love and healing spells.

Cingulum, the long cord is tied with nine knots. It is in these knots where the cingulum's power is. When they are braided, they can be used for binding rituals, casting sacred circles or for making weather spells and determining a circle's circumference.

Crystal Ball Crystal Ball utilized since the beginning of the 19th century by fortune tellers and witches as a powerful divination instrument. It's not as popular in the present, but it's useful in witchcraft. It's a globe-shaped object made out of a crystal and it is available in various shades. It is associated with femininity and water. It is also used for the spirit of summoning and shamanic communications. Crystal balls are an investment that is costly, and it is no wonder that they're not as sought-after as Tarot cards. When they are not in use, crystal ball are covered with cloth or stored in a dark box, and cleaned with magical washes as well as incense smoke and floral-infused spring water.

Horns and Cornucopias Horns and Cornucopias: These are placed on the altar and are used to summon spirits. A few

Wiccan sects make use of the Horn as a chalice in rituals. It can also be used to secure caps at times of celebrations when the High Priest is impersonating the Horned God.

Masks: Made of clay, crystals, wood and feathers, hemp stone, papier mache and other materials, they function as sacred portals that grant the wearer access to the realm of magic. They also provide protection from the evil forces, function as talismans or shields, as well as receptacles to a supernatural power. Masks are used to cover faces of the dead and also as votive offerings. In the medieval period witches were able to wear masks that were full or half-masks to protect their anonymity and prevent the possibility of being captured.

Mirrors: Mirrors of today are made of glass. Mirrors from the past were made of copper which was polished until it turned reflective. Mirrors are utilized in protection spells and love magic, as well as scrying, as well as spirit summoning. They are often associated with gods such as Oshun, Venus, and Hathor and are used in various religions, most notably Aztec, Celtic, and folk magic.

Mortar and pestle Often described as an instrument for transportation that was witchy The mortar and pestle were once primary grinding tools. In witchcraft, they're employed in the crushing of plants and creating ointments that are used for various uses. Modern tools are used to accomplish the same thing but this mortar has a symbolic meaning since it brings you in contact with your magic materials and your desired goals in ways that the press of a button is not able to replicate. The tejolote and molcajete made of volcanic rock are the most traditional Mexican mortars and pestles used by witches. Nowadays, they are constructed out of glass, marble as well as brass, stone and Terracotta.

Pentacle: a fundamental Wiccan instrument that symbolizes Earth element. Pentacles are used to act as an emblem an amulet or talisman as the cross does the symbol for Christians as well as the hexagram to the Jews. The earliest pentacle is dated to around 4000 CE.

Singing Bowls: An amalgam of seven different metals (gold antimony, mercury, copper, silver iron, tin and) placed on an altar in order to attract harmony from the cosmic energy in the form of sound. This helps to cleanse the space, tune the chakras, and aid in the process of astral travel and spellwork.

Stang: A wooden two-pronged staff that is used for Wiccan rituals. "Stang" is a Wiccan word "stang" can be described as an ancient Norse word that refers to poles or staff. The bifurcations of the stang symbolize the Horns from the Horned God. Stangs are employed in casting spells and summoning spirits. They also function as a compass when they are placed in the north of a sacred circle , and as a center of energy to direct it. It is possible to make your own with a elm branch and magnolia, ash, and a knife for carving.

Wand: This refers to the element of fire and typically is six inches long but you can alter the length to suit your needs. The first wands were made of wood and were made of willow, yew and oak tree. Hazel is the ideal wood to make wands from then willow or ash cut in the waxing or full moon. Nowadays, wands can be made from metal or glass and decorated with stones. They can be used for the drawing of energy or in directing it. Contrary to those in the Harry Potter franchise, you pick the wand you want to use. The feeling will fill your tummy when you've found the one that is right for you. But, the wand is unfilled till you fill it up with energy and determination.

Feel free to make the tools you want to use if have metal forging or carpentry abilities. If you decide to purchase one, inquire about the history of the tool and ensure that it's not stained by blood.

Clean and Storing the Magical Instruments

Crystals and tools are cleansed using holy water created by mixing spring water with sea salt under the full moon. Crystals, as with other magical instruments, absorb energy thoughts, emotions, and thoughts for a lengthy period of time. There are many methods to cleanse them.

Conclusion

If you're here, I'm assuming you have read this book from completely to explore the many facets of witchcraft and occultism. It is now clear that understanding the supernatural requires conviction, a clear mind, a desire to persevere, patience, and the determination to carry out along with the ability to take the full responsibility for any step you take under the guise of mysticism.

You'll be able to make solid arguments in situations where you must defend your new ideas about supernatural events or the usage of magical techniques. Witches and occultists don't abuse children, ride with brooms or change their appearance to any shape they want. They do not belong to fairy stories. They are alive breathing human beings, and everywhere you look.

Witchcraft is popular with us all since it tackles important issues, such as the challenge of overcoming religious bias as well as environmental care and gender equality as well as the dangers of simplistic thinking. The witches as well as Wiccans alike have a single primary aim in mind: improving themselves and the world , while doing their part to improve the world through magic. They do this with the understanding that their actions have an impact on all things and everyone else.

Magic is everywhere around you. When you travel this path, utilize all the knowledge you have gained in this book to tap the power of your own. The realms beyond physical reality will always be available to you, so you will gain the experience. You'll notice that this book delves into the flowery language that is found in a lot of texts and provides specific methods to practice magic. There is no correct or incorrect method to become a witch, therefore be proud of your work and listen to the witchy snarl. Take off your besom and fly.

It is important to keep a sense of authenticity for you when you are practicing your craft. Every witch is unique. It is this distinctiveness and authenticity that lies at the center of witchcraft. The books can only get you only so far. If you're looking to make a move take it, then take the step. Fear will not stop you. What's the most likely thing that can occur? You get a spell wrong? Aren't we been there before? The art of magic is trial and error for 90 times out of the day. It is only through constant practice that you can increase your confidence in your abilities , and will increase your spiritual connection.

Don't stop studying. Let the universe guide you as you chart your own path to fulfillment. Be ethical and never forget the Wiccan Rede, which tells us not to make use of our abilities to hurt another. Wicca can change your life. As you develop your craft, you'll grow and learn from others , and effortlessly incorporate new abilities throughout your life. Merry greetings, happy part and blessed be!

www.ingramcontent.com/pod-product-compliance
Lightning Source LLC
Chambersburg PA
CBHW050407120526